A problem well put is half-solved. The reactionary is a man of few words, well-chosen, which cut to the heart of a problem. In the history of ideas there have been works which have laid bare the problems of modernity, and whose elegance has pointed the way to their solution.

Imperium Press' Studies in Reaction series distills the essence of reactionary thought. The series presents in compact format those seminal works which need so few words to say so much about modernity.

JONATHAN BOWDEN was a British orator, painter, and novelist. Beginning his political career as a member of the Conservative Party, he co-founded the Revolutionary Conservative Caucus and quarterly journal *The Revolutionary Conservative Review* before joining the British National Party. A towering intellect with an encyclopaedic knowledge of illiberal thought both left and right, Bowden earned a reputation for powerful oratory, quickly becoming a fixture on the far right speaking circuit. Since his premature death aged 49, his reputation has continued to grow, and he is now considered a seminal figure in what has come to be known as the alt right, and subsequent dissident right movements.

WHY
I AM NOT
A LIBERAL

JONATHAN
BOWDEN

PERTH
IMPERIUM PRESS
2020

Published by Imperium Press

www.imperiumpress.org

Interview conducted by Black Gnosis
Transcription courtesy of Counter Currents Publishing
The moral rights of all parties have been asserted
Used under license to Imperium Press

FIRST EDITION

A catalogue record for this
book is available from the
National Library of Australia

ISBN 978-0-6488593-0-7 Paperback
ISBN 978-0-6488593-1-4 EPUB
ISBN 978-0-6488593-2-1 Kindle

CONTENTS

Acknowledgements and Dedication

The editor wishes to acknowledge, above all, the late Jonathan Bowden. This is a fitting first title for the Studies in Reaction series, being comprised of pithy reactionary works, as Bowden himself acted as a gateway to illiberal right intellectuals by his précis of them. This little volume is dedicated to him.

The editor also wishes to acknowledge Black Gnosis, whose members not only had the foresight to record many of Bowden's talks and to interview him, but who also granted permission to republish all content that follows.

Finally, he wishes to acknowledge Counter Currents, who, in addition to doing important work in their own right, have granted permission to use their transcription of this interview.

A Note From the Interviewer

The following is a transcript of a three and a half hour interview I filmed with the British author, artist, and orator, Jonathan Bowden, back in 2009.

The location was a bar in a private members' club for ex/serving military personnel, in Waterloo central London.

Sat surrounding Bowden, in a horseshoe shape, like attentive listening disciples around a besuited sage were fifteen members of the *London New-Right*; the pragmatic English take on France's *GRECE/Nouvelle-Droite*, that was founded in 2005 by Troy Southgate. The interview itself had taken place shortly after Bowden had closed a successful NR meeting with a memorable and energetic talk about the historical and cultural significance of *Punch & Judy*; a favourite subject he'd covered previously in essays and a film entitled *Grand Guignol*.

Forever the performer, Bowden enjoyed the attention and answered the myriad of questions put to him instantaneously, like an actor delivering lines from a well rehearsed script, but in his case, they were questions he had been contemplating for most of his adult life. The topics ranged from a damning critique of The Conservative party, UKIP (*United Kingdom Independence Party*) the BNP (*British National Party*), Islam, Christianity, Paganism, the Middle-East, Israel, the EU, Feminism, and the social decline of the working-class ethnic-English in the post-industrial north.

In-between questioning we broke for coffee and I decided to keep the camera running. For myself, this was the most interesting part of the whole proceedings because it allowed Jonathan's humour, complaisance, and knowledge of British popular culture and subcultures to come through. There were also some humourous anecdotes thrown in about an ex-tabloid newspaper columnist and characters that Bowden had crossed paths with over the years. Due to their potentially libellous nature I promised Jonathan I would edit them out if the interview ever saw the light of day.

> *Cut all that stuff out I said about G—y Bu—ll, would*
> *you?*

As is now widely known Jonathan passed away in March of 2012 from coronary failure—not long after suffering a nervous breakdown—and a month shy of his 50th birthday. As was commented about his death elsewhere online, "when you push your mind to those sorts of limits something has to give". Jonathan Bowden, a Nietzschean 'til the end.

Work and Legacy

With the sad passing of Jonathan Bowden the New Right has lost one of its most gifted advocates and humanity has lost its most gifted orator. Like other commentators who have written about Jonathan in the few weeks since the announcement of his death, I regard Jonathan's unique contribution to have been his erudite, entertaining and inspiring speeches. Whilst there is no substitute for hearing a great speaker in the flesh, it is happily true that a great deal of the power of Jonathan's oratory is communicated through the many videos that were made of his talks, and which are currently available to view online. This enduring legacy is largely due to the foresight of a Black Gnosis member, who took the trouble to film many of Jonathan's speeches at the regular London New Right gatherings.

I first became aware of the power of Jonathan's oratory when someone on an internet forum asked Troy Southgate if the transcript of a particular speech could be made available. Troy replied that Jonathan never prepared or consulted notes when he spoke. This intrigued me. In the modern world of endless noise and distraction how many people have the mental capacity to deliver an hour long speech without notes or preparation? When I found the speech in question online and listened to it, my intrigue grew to an immense respect. 'Heidegger and Death's Ontology' taught me a great deal about Heidegger, a philosopher I had found too daunting to ever try reading, and it inspired me to begin exploring his work. It also taught me a great deal about Jonathan: about his encyclopaedic knowledge; about the laser precision of his eloquence; and about his ability to enrapture an audience with a forbiddingly abstruse topic.

The facility with which he could engage his listeners was remarkable to behold. All the more so considering the fact that he never talked down to an audience. Indeed, he expected his audience to do a great deal of work in following his various trains of thought, his labyrinthine sub clauses, and his perfectly formulated parentheses. The complicated structural form of his talks was never a barrier to understanding them; it just seemed to be a necessary means to incorporate the vast array of ideas and illustrations that were required for him to express what he had to say. And what he chose to emphasize again and again was that we are engaged in a cultural struggle at all levels of social activity.

One example of this will suffice. During one particular speech Jonathan claimed that Pol Pot, the future leader of the Khmer Rouge, heard lectures given at the Sorbonne by Jean ·Paul Sartre and Simone de Beauvoir. When these existentialist intellectuals discussed notions such as the necessity of destroying the family as a bourgeois construct, Pol Pot interpreted them rather literally and carried out their ideas with Maoist zeal. Thus, Jonathan described a political spectrum of Marxism stretching from the feminism of The Second Sex to the killing fields of Cambodia. And this, of course, is the dirty secret of liberalism. When it requires a face of tolerance and humanity to succeed then it will wear that face; when it requires bullets, the mask is changed accordingly. The hypocrisy is mostly hidden due to the hegemonic influence of the Left across all political and cultural institutions.

Jonathan often described the New Right as an alternative university, one free from this hegemony of Marxism. His desire was to see everyone on the New Right raise their game and begin to address these cultural issues directly from our perspective. To a great extent this is a lesson that has to be learned from the praxis of the New Left. We are at a stage where political censorship and demographic change have made it impossible (or at least unlikely, if one is being optimistic) for us to regain control of our political institutions by the usual channels. The role of the New Right, as Jonathan delineated it, is to explore the realm of ideas at a higher level; to face the intellectual reality of New Left hegemony and challenge it head on; and to provide a cultural space wherein young people, whose ideas may not yet have been totally corrupted, can find an alternative current to the materialistic doctrines of contemporary Western societies. This is a project that can and should be pursued at all levels of cultural activity. Whether in the creation of fine art; the reviewing of popular films; or the exegesis of complex philosophical ideas, we should be attuned to our position as European men and women resisting the current of materialism and liberalism.

Jonathan pursued this cultural project vigorously, producing a great many paintings and books, and also a couple of films. It is true that some of these works are difficult to locate within a conventional 'right wing' discourse, but I do not think that this is a failure of those works. Instead, they represent a desire to create a new aesthetic space in which works which are expressive of the ethos of Western man could be produced, without the necessity of either craven apologetics to the liberal elite or self-imposed submission to a didacticism of the right. His paintings in particular, which look like a sort of cross between Egon Schiele and Francis Bacon gone wrong, can seem deeply rooted in post-modernity, but in reality they express a sense of projection into a more autonomous artistic future. The distortion of the figures and the claustrophobia of the composition are relieved by the vivacity of the colour palate and an associated sense of strength and belief. I believe that many of these pictures represent the caging and etherization of the European spirit at the present time and the ultimate indefatigability of that spirit, and I suspect that they will come to be more admired as time goes on.

Whenever Jonathan spoke in public he wore a wooden runic pendant to express his pagan beliefs. The symbol on the pendant was the odal, or eðel, rune. This is representative of 'home' or 'homeland'. A home is a space that is won by one's ancestors and that must be vigorously defended by the descendants or it will be destroyed. Within the home it is possible to be oneself, to experience a real and hard-won sense of authenticity and autonomy. But the price for this is constant vigilance. The integrity of our Western homelands has now been breached; the causes for this are manifold, and so the methods of our resurgence must be manifold. This seems to me to encapsulate Jonathan's weltanschauung, and to provide a blueprint for us to continue to manifest his legacy.

Christopher Pankhurst, 2012

Jonathan Bowden: A Memorial

Ladies and gentlemen/Meine Damen und Herren,

As I'm fond of telling people, I used to attend Theosophical meetings in Letchworth. There in large letters across the front of the stage was the legend, "There's no religion higher than truth". So what I'm going to do today is to tell the truth about Jonathan Bowden.

As Jonathan would have concurred, there is at heart two kinds of truth. There are the truths we feel inside ourselves and there are the outside truths which we discover through impartial observation. The inside truths are the emotional values we give to things and which are of our very essence, while the outside truths represent the factual reality by which we have to live. In fact, although separate, we depend on finding an equilibrium between both kinds of truth for our survival. Yet, however we regard truth, it's my contention here that Jonathan Bowden's memory, above all others, can withstand the spotlight of truth.

During his life Jonathan was a complete enigma, a mystery which is only now beginning to unravel since his death. Those of us who knew him well were never invited to his home—except in my case at the very end—after his breakdown. And those of us who enjoyed the privilege of his company on a one to one basis, often through driving him around the country, will recall that on dropping him off he would sometimes walk in a different direction to throw us off the scent as to where he actually lived. Now, after his death, though, I think we should respect his dignity and not speculate over much as to the reasons for such subterfuge. The best thing to do is to recognize that while not only was Jonathan an intensely private man, above all, as I shall explain, he also created his own reality.

He was fond of referring to Mycroft, the fictitious Sherlock Holmes' fictitious brother. A character who was virtually a disembodied brain having only a tentative connection with physical reality. Like Mycroft, Jonathan existed largely through his own thoughts and imagination. The material world, apart from a sometimes hearty appetite, was almost extraneous to his life. On many of our long walks beside the River Thames, I would be brimming over with wonderment at the variety and beauty of nature, wanting to share my joy of the outside world with him, but although never unappreciative, Jonathan's eyes would always remain firmly fixed on the conundrums within his mind. Side by side with Jonathan's intellectual understanding was the joyful wisdom brought to him through his intellectual courage; courage to face objective truth and so conquer new realms of knowledge. Jonathan epitomised the Aryan tradition because like Prometheus he dared steal fire from heaven.

When I first got to know Jonathan well I would ferry him around on the back of my motorbike which is all I had in those days. Sitting pillion with his large furled, golfing umbrella, wearing my spare crash helmet (which would never have passed the health and safety commissars) and completely fearless as we winged our way around country lanes, he always reminded me of some Don Quixote tilting at windmills. Perhaps we both were!

It was only once I'd bought a car that I started to drive Jonathan to political meetings and it was in his speeches that he displayed his complete disregard, contempt even, for political temporizing. Asked on a Red White and Blue platform whether he was an ethno-nationalist he replied, that he wouldn't lie to the British people; he was a racial nationalist! On another occasion, in front of the assembled British National Party leadership he would declare for the "Aryan Race". Nick Griffin's thoughts were palpable, "We've got a right one here", I could hear him thinking. Or we may recall how Jonathan upset Party functionaries for instance, by asserting at a meeting in the North West that he was a Fascist and White Supremacist! Shocking though such sentiments may seem (well to some people anyway) Jonathan would reason—how can we attract a leadership corps, how can we appeal to a much needed new elite if we refuse to take honest cognizance of our historical context? Furthermore, how can we take our country back for the White British people if the White British people are not supreme in their own land? Without White supremacy "British jobs for British workers" is just a hollow phrase.

Jonathan Bowden, we miss you!

Yet there was no trace of pettiness in Jonathan's attitude towards other races or anything else for that matter. Behind his assumed Nietzschean facade was a very sensitive and understanding person. Not for him conspiracy theories either, whether true or untrue. Jonathan saw life only as an idealistic battle of ideas: between elitism and liberalism, between aspiration and degeneracy; not between vested interests, Zionist, financial or otherwise. If he were ever a materialist it would have been of the ethereal variety!

In every way Jonathan stood leftist presumptions on their head. Take the liberal idea of tabula rasa for example—the idea that as individuals we are completely innocent. Our brains are a clean slate upon which our experience and upbringing writes its unique story and shapes our character. Yes! Jonathan looked at his own tabula rasa as a completely clean slate, but, instead of allowing the chance happenings of the outside world to write his story, he would assume complete control. He would write his own fictitious story. Jonathan decided from an early age to write his own life story.

That doesn't mean that real things never happened to him, of course they did, but his creative imagination allowed him to recreate, reinvent himself. He recreated himself as the principal protagonist in his own novel. Although I suspect his breakdown eventually proved his undoing, his first words to me after he realised what was happening were, "Good, just like Nietzsche!"

As Jonathan's medication gradually allowed the outside world to replace his inside world so it shattered his life's creation. Those who saw him more recently could tell that whilst he had lost none of his intellectual vigour, he had lost some of his old confidence. Some of the ghost had already left the machine.

Many of our circle are courageous. (I can think of more than one in this room today). As individuals we defy conventional norms as dealt to us by a degenerate society. But, Jonathan Bowden was unique in that he detached himself entirely from the contemporary world of dross and compromise to reinvent himself as his own hero. A true romantic, and for us a true hero also. Thank you.

Michael Woodbridge, London Forum, April 19th, 2012

WHY
I AM NOT
A LIBERAL

Right. So, it's sort of like a Star Chamber, isn't it? Oh dear, they're all waiting, hungry to feed upon the carcass.

So, Jonathan, why aren't you a liberal?

I think, basically, because liberalism is not a three-dimensional view of life. I don't think it's at all deep or at all sincere.

The real reason is quite personal, actually, because my mother died when I was 16, and was insane before she died, and it struck me that the ways in which people would talk about this and deal with anything profound or anything tragic or anything real or that punctures through the superficial mask that people wear about things in our society now, was so trivial and materialistic and silly that I couldn't go along with it.

And so, my first views, even the liberal sort, were a reaction against the tendentious propositions that liberalism enfolds: everything's material; all people are equal; all lives are equally important; tragedy is largely fictional; "grin and bear it." Do you remember the Panglossian sort of attitude that you get in Voltaire's *Candide*? You know, everything's always for the best and this sort of utterly trivial and, in one sense, irreligious attitude towards life just sort of nauseated and appalled me. I thought that there has to be something better than this.

Many people who aren't liberals become communists, Marxists. You didn't feel drawn towards those ideologies?

No, because I've always believed in human inequality. I believe human inequality is the basis of life, but also the basis of morality, because I believe inequality is a moral force. The real division between the Left and Right is not about people who support socialized medicine or even much more harsh measures, if you like, or divisive measures like ethnicity or abortion or whatever. The real division, philosophically, is those who believe that equality, enforced or otherwise, is a moral good (broadly the general Left) and those who believe—and are often are too frightened to say so—that inequality is a moral good, which is what the philosophical Right really believes in.

Even the most moderate center-Right figure, the John Majors of this world, talk about freedom, opportunity. If you have opportunity, you'll have inequality even in a Marxian system. So, although they're frightened to mention the I-word, if you like, all Rightist movements from the most moderate to the most radical, right across the spectrum, believe that inequality is inescapable, is a fact, has to be lived through, has to be dealt with, and is actually the way things should be.

So, the idea that you can engineer society through radical shifts or change, so as to create more equality, is to me completely counter-propositional. I remember Trotsky once said, before he teamed up with Lenin again just prior to the Bolshevik *coup*—which is what it really was—that once socialism has been established, once there's a reign of equality for all at the level of material subsistence and beyond (education, health, and other matters) there will be a Goethe on every street corner; he said there will be a Kant on every street corner; there'll be a Strindberg on every corner. Notice all these more gentile, Caucasian cultural heroes. There will be one of these on every street corner.

That's utter nonsense. Genius like that is against the grain, is largely hated while it's alive, by many people, but revered after it's gone. These people are extraordinarily difficult for others to get a handle on while they actually exist. They're freaks of nature, sort of "special needs" the other way around. The idea that such an outcome could be pre-programmed by socially enforced engineering that presses *down* upon the difference between people rather than seeks to exalt is completely counter-propositional.

So, the moral ideas that lie behind Marxism and socialism, Left-democratic socialism, Left-liberalism, and so on as you come in from the ultra-Left to the center, never interested me.

Anarchism or individualistic ideas sort of, in a Nietzschean way, would interest me a bit more, but the idea of the moral goodness of equality never interested me at all.

So, Marxism and its offshoots would never be for me, although there is one area where I respect them and that's their commitment to theory, their commitment, not to debate, but to ideas, and their belief that the world can be changed, and their seriousness of purpose, because all Tories in the world, and ninnies and fools, they never believed that these people are serious, they never believed that they were *deadly* serious in their humorlessness, in their ranting, in their dialectic, in what they wanted to enforce. They were completely serious, and the sort of "reactionary" view that they could be laughed at and scorned, which was largely the reaction to the 1960s for example, in certain respects, has been proved to be totally false. The cultural values are such that these people have taken over, and people who call themselves conservative are all at sea and don't even know what's happened.

You yourself were a conservative for a while or at least were in the Conservative Party. Tell us about those times.

There's a two-party system in Britain. My view is it's one party with two wings and a fulcrum, and the two wings (bourgeois proletarian, center-Left, center-Right, red and blue) switch around it. Nevertheless, from the south of England the bourgeois party of power, the mechanism of government, a semi-totalitarian power in parts of the southeast, is the Conservative Party, so I joined that and was attracted to things like the Monday Club on its Right wing.

The one thing I've noticed about that type of conservatism though is, as Revilo P. Oliver once said, "Conservatism is not enough." And the problem with it is manifold. In the British tradition in particular, it's very philistine; it's very anti-intellectual; it's a-theoretical; it's pragmatic. It's also quite afraid. It's afraid of the doctrine of respectability. Tories are obsessed with being respectable, obsessed with being thought nice. It's of no moment as far as I'm concerned. They've got a fear of the disapproval of their bourgeois peers which is semi-traumatic.

The center-Left would always use the ideas of the extreme Left even if it repudiates the politics. You can repudiate Leninism and the ideas of utter ruthlessness and the ends justify the means, and yet at the same time you can believe in radical socialist postulates, whereas the moderate Right is terrified, libertarianism aside, from using the ideas of the radical Right. I think that's its great weakness, that it won't even accept the ideas that would allow one to fight back, and that's why they've been completely outmaneuvered and virtually culturally destroyed.

What's left of intellectual conservatism now? It's almost done. Michael Oakeshott and these sorts of people are a distant memory; Professor Maurice Cowling is dead; Scruton has partly fallen silent at least in terms of media exposure in comparison to when I was younger. Because, you see, if you were to confront this society now as a radical conservative—if such a thing is possible—you would have to use radical Right ideas, and they won't go there. They won't touch them, and they're deeply frightened. Even if they put it in the form of Guillaume Faye, Alain de Benoist, or whatever. Even that is too much.

What will inevitably follow is that certainly the realm with ideas they've gone now, in a confused way, just sort of collapsed into the general liberal slough, and more radical forces will have to represent the sorts of views that you would have expected them to uphold in the past. But maybe it was always a fallacy to believe that they would uphold them.

Why have they not fought back? Why have they had this problem with not accepting the ideas of the radical Right and using them?

Too conformist, too bourgeois, too afraid, too unintellectual, too snobbish, too materially comfortable. All those sorts of views. Different for each individual within the spectrum, of course. Somebody else will always do it. Reversing many of the processes of decline will involve roughness and a degree of possible nastiness. Such politics will inevitably involve the working class and involve a large swathe of the population that they would rather not associate with, politicize in relation to. The whole point of much of their politics is in a sense to keep that group out of the political process to a degree. Therefore, to deal with the decline on their watch involves such radical reshaping of one's mind that, in a way, they're not up for it.

Is it not also the case that cultural controllers, being at the Left, have got the means of demonizing them so much that they fear being isolated?

Yes, there's also that, but the idea of respectability is part and parcel of the avoidance of demonization. I think I once said in a talk that the Tory leader when I was born was Douglas-Home. You couldn't imagine him being a member, no matter how honorary, of United Against Fascism. Cameron is alleged to be a member of United Against Fascism. I have no idea whether he is or not or whether it's just a powerful media spin. Nevertheless, the very idea that he could even be thought of as a member of that group in comparison to conservative leaders of the past, even just for social reasons, is totally absurd. And that shows you that they're riven with fear about the things which 50 years ago they would have regarded as normal and natural.

Are there any conservative members, any conservative leaders, members of parliament that you met in your time with them who impressed you?

Yes, there was some of that old British generation, partly because politics is generational, and before the war there was a generation of people who were around well into the '60s; a few didn't die until late in the '70s; there's a few around even into the early 1980s, but they were very old men then. Some people like Julian Amery and so on who would never have known me, although I attended meetings where he spoke back when I was a teenager and he was a very old man. Ronald Bell. These sorts of people. Amery's an interesting man, related to Louis Amery, who wrote the six-volume biography of Joseph Chamberlain. They were quite close to Enoch Powell. John Amery, of course, was hanged for treason at the end of the war and was a member of his family. He invited Giorgio Almirante when Almirante was the leader of the Italian Social Movement over to the Tory conference once. That caused a bit of a stir. So, that element was there, but it was a dying element. It was essentially anti-communist, and the Cold War was raging, so it's understandable. But they didn't want to think out of the box.

Again, there's an absence of radicalism in the thinking, undue concern with respectability and being thought to be on the right side, the view that if capitalism triumphs everything will be all right and the view that if Soviet Communism was defeated everything would be all right. You can see why many would think that, but also as things have turned out those were very, very shallow views, and the world that they really believed in has disappeared, because they were not prepared to think more radically about the world that they were in and the fact that it was changing all around them even when they were still middle-aged to early old age and could still be mentally youthful.

So, the death of conservatism is intellectual and moral death whether the center-Right here or Christian Democracy in Europe or any intellectuality within the Republican Party in the United States. It's all part of a package. The center-Right is bereft and valueless. If Cameron could be honestly debated with, if such a thing is possible, what does he actually stand for above spinning and being a Tory Blair and managing the decline a bit more efficaciously than Brown?

What's your view of UKIP?

Politically, it's quite important. Ideologically, I despise UKIP, but politically it's quite important because they've broken the middle class bloc. For many conservative, middle class southern English people in particular, voting UKIP is a radical gesture, and although many hardliners would sneer at that, for them it's a truth. To break away from the blue to the purple and yellow is not insignificant.

UKIP's divided into two sections as far as I can see. A half of them are Right-wing liberals who are libertarians, who are fanatically pro-market and pro-United States, who would like to leave the European Union and join the North Atlantic Treaty Organization and would therefore really just swap one federation for another. Half of them are sympathetic to the far Right, often in a sort of bourgeois way, but they are. So, I think it's half and half and you ought to take the half that is. If you can break them off you will get more populist far Right Euro-MPs, you will get much more influence, you will push further into the right flank of where the Tories were. You will also combine middle class votes with working class votes. So, they are part of the synthesis.

How is that done? Could it be done?

The middle class has to see people who are like themselves, and they will not vote for a working class movement in my opinion. It's not so much that they want to see soft or reflexive or nice people, but they want to see people that they can identify with. My view is that as long as they're not seen to be insane, how radical they are is less important.

European countries have a far Right tradition, respectable far Right tradition, but Britain does not have this. Why, in your opinion, is this so?

I think there is such a tradition, but it's virtually got lost, and there was nothing really to continue it. In France, you have this range of intellectuals in a very radical environment. Don't forget, these people either collaborated during the war with Vichy or did not, they were rather pure nationalists like Maurras, who stayed in his house and even the Resistance couldn't guillotine him at the end of the war because he detested the Germans and didn't collaborate. But most of them did collaborate and Robert Brasillach was guillotined for collaborating, and Drieu La Rochelle committed suicide for collaborating, and so on.

But the intellectual tradition in France survived partly because of a greater degree of intellectual radicalism. You have a culture that teaches philosophy from the age of 6, whereas most British people would be pushed to tell you what philosophy was. Therefore, there's a degree to which you're dealing with a different sort of culturalization. You also have extreme Leftists become extreme Rightists in a way that's very rare in Britain.

It's not an anti-intellectual or philistine culture at all. It's just that it has a different attitude towards intellectuality. It privatized it a long time ago. Intellectuals do what they do over there in this little zone, and as long as they don't cause trouble you can almost have as much freedom of speech as you want.

All of these laws that have been passed to prevent freedom of speech: if you put things in an abstract way, no one can touch you. But the masses don't even know what you're talking about and so you just talk to tiny little groups on your own. But that's the definition of British intellectuality.

If you look at the British/English far Right tradition, you have this range of Americans at the early part of the 20th century who come over with the New English sensibility: Canadian-born Wyndham Lewis; you have Ezra Pound; you have T. S. Eliot. They're largely literary figures, but you do have Raven Thomson, who's a sort of fascistic theorist around Mosley; you have Mosley himself, who is quite a considerable theorist; you have people like Bill Hopkins after the war, who's hardly known but is there and is known of inside the intelligentsia; you have the Right edge of the Angry Young Men phenomenon, which is a media created thing and is largely synthetic. But in some ways the tradition does sort of die out there. You have Henry Williamson on either side of the war. But after him there's a gap, you see, because there's no really coherent movement. You have the emergence of revisionist historians like David Irving. That's true. David Irving was initially thought to have been Left-wing, of course, when Kimber published *The Destruction of Dresden*, because traditionally only Leftists would decry Allied activities in the war, you see, and that was actually quite a clever move by

Irving as well. It was only later that people learned the "full horror," allegedly.

But, yes, there is a gap. But then of course how many great intellectual conservatives are there? Oakeshott, Cowling, Scruton, a few sort of intermediate minds, a few literati, like the diarist Alan Clark. Most military historians are conservative, of course, because they're slightly authoritarian psychologically and like the military. Even a moderate figure like Max Hastings, who's made extensive work of Irving's researches, of course, although that's not that widely known. But there are enough people. It's not many, admittedly. You'd fill about a shelf in terms of books, but not many.

But there is an intellectual tradition here. If there had been a lively discourse of that sort on the edge of the Conservative Party, there'd probably have been more. But many of them have hidden, they've denied what their views really were or they've gone from communism to clubland reaction like Kingsley Amis, who begins as a Leftist and ends as a bit of a clubbable bore, really, whiskey in hand, sort of *Daily Mail* rantings at the end.

But intellectually I don't think that's very important. It's a change of mind. I remember John Braine the famous author from the '50s wrote a pamphlet called "From the Communist Party to the Monday Club".[1] And the Monday Club used to sell it. It was one of the pamphlets that I bought from them when I joined it as a very young man. "From the Communist Party to the Monday Club." You see, it's a sort of . . . It's something, but it's not quite enough. It's almost symptomatic of the fact that Braine had made it, a penniless writer makes it from the north of England.

No, it's not enough. I put it down to fear and the jaundiced palsy of conservatism. Conservatives are deeply decent people on one level, but they're afraid, terribly afraid, and of what they're not quite sure but they know that they're afraid enough not to wish to be unrespectable.

So, of course, the next question is why aren't you yourself afraid?

I don't know. You'll have to do genetic tests. But probably because I'm too extreme, because I've got radical attitudes. There's an intensely conservative side to me, but I'm probably a bohemian. There's an artistic element in me. I don't care for

1 Actually, "*Goodbye to the Left*".

bourgeois respectability. It doesn't bother me. That's where the leaders of the extreme Right often come from. They actually come from the arts as much as from the academy or from the intelligentsia, and the arts are a psychologically very radical part of the society, and therefore you don't care as much for, you know, being regarded as a bit of a demon.

And how can we nurture more of these people? How can we renew the radical Right?

By making it exciting, by making it the oppositional force within the culture, by saying that it's no longer the Left, that the Left has died. You know, The History Man caricatured by Bradbury and so on in the '70s based upon a particular Jewish liberal Left academic called Laurie Taylor. That's dead now. All that culture. Marching with your fist in the air at Essex University. All that sort of stuff. It's all over now, and any energy of opposition will come from the other side.

And it's true. I remember there's a bar in Maidenhead in the middle of Berkshire, it's gone bust now, but it used to be called the Soviet Bar and you used to be able to go in there and have a Dzerzhinsky, who was the founder of the Soviet secret police, the Cheka. Have a Dzerzhinsky! There wouldn't be a bar where you could go in and have a Himmler! And that's because the Soviet Union . . . You know those posters on tube stations? The masses . . . spectacles with a red banner in the background and all this. All of this Soviet iconography could be reused in the capitalist marketplace.

Situationism is a theory that's 40 years old now where everything can be reused; it can be recycled; everything's absorbed into the system of 24-hour media. But there are two things that can't be absorbed: the extreme Right and religious fundamentalism, as it's called, can't be absorbed. Those two can't be absorbed. Everything revolves around that, and that makes them very exciting, of course, sometimes for the wrong reasons.

More people will come forward when it becomes the normal oppositional current. But what will change the view isn't fashionability, and isn't accessibility, it's morality. For a significant proportion of the generations born after the Second World War, radical Right-wing positions, they believe, are instinctually immoral. Because they did not think that before 1939. It was dissident, but it was another political position. That's not the case afterwards. The reason for people not wanting to be unrespectable is partly moral respectability. When you break through that, you will tap the idealism that goes into Green politics, that goes into anti-federalism, that goes into politics about animals, and all these other slightly peripheral things. In some ways it's an ethical question. If you can break through that barrier the idealism of the young and others is there for you, but I don't think you'll get large numbers of people until that happens.

Liberals, Marxists, the enemies of the radical Right control television, they control movies, they control the media, they control everything worth controlling, everything that molds the minds of the young. How do we combat this?

The internet is the way to combat it, because the internet will gradually eat all those structures, and they will have to go on it in order to survive. So, the internet which couldn't be stopped and is based on American military technology from yesteryear, is that which will come to eat the controlling methodology which now superintends media. I think there was a pop band in the 1980s called Pop Will Eat Itself, and the internet is sort of the media devouring itself and becoming something different. Under 30 years of age, the only media they look at is the internet, because they can see all the old media on the internet anyway, so they just go to the net. And you can have obscure meetings with people, and it can be seen millions of times on the internet, if you have something that is regarded as worth listening to. Now, of course, the internet contains utter trash. It's everything that the human mind has ever encompassed. So, you've got the worst and the best that humans can do on it and depicted on it, but that's just really an electronic simulacrum of the human brain and its potentials for good or ill. So, the internet will break it and has largely done already. It's uncontrollable, even though the authorities can come down, and they can look at what's on your hard drive even when you don't know they're doing it, even when you're on the computer. Because there are no secrets in that world, you see. But at the same time it's completely broken liberal propaganda, and in the end they know that, and they all look at it as well. You know, why does Melanie Phillips write about me in *The Spectator*? Because she knows. Because *The Spectator* is never going to employ me to write for them, not now anyway, but she knows.

Although there was a chance maybe if I had taken a different course, if I had began the process of lying from an early stage, which in order to become a major Tory you have to do. When the management committee says "Are you in favor of the death penalty?" you've got to say no to get to the next stage. And then they say "Are you in favor of further EU integration?" And you say "Well, you know, I'd rather keep sovereignty here." And the old ladies on the committee—the Madame Defarges of the shires—will nod, you know, but already you're temporizing, you're sort of playing the game, you're moving inside, you're always saying what the listener wants to hear so you can go on to the next stage, because if you don't you'll be excluded. What's the point of trying to be included if you behave as to make yourself excluded?

What about ethnic politics? Would you say politics is ethnic?

No. Yes, I remember someone on the extreme Right once said that they didn't think I was a "racist." Well, that's odd isn't it? Because that's the worst thing you can be called in the contemporary liberal society. But my views are, I'm a Nietzschean, and my views are philosophical. Race is a primary identity out of which culture comes, and without which you can't sustain a civilization, but I personally believe that it is the going *up* from that which is rooted and that which is physical, that life is really about.

So, there's always a socialism in totally racialist movements, whereas for me it is a hierarchy that is based upon something. A tree has roots, grows out of the ground, goes up towards the sun and a healthy atmosphere, water on the tree and so on, it grows out and the branches mushroom, and it's a healthy plant organism. But it's growing upwards towards something. In the end, race is a materialism. But because the whole of the liberal Left consensus denies that it is foundational to create civic structure they've based societies on considerable lies.

They've also opened the door to the demographic doom of their own group, in part or in whole, and they've also made a cardinal mistake about the nature of civilization, because you will inevitably water down—maybe not quite, but almost to nothingness—the culture you can create if you deny that there is a physical basis to life.

But there is a physical basis to life. A child that's born without limbs is a physical basis to life. Madness is physiological. Perversion is physiological. Physical excellence is physiological. Beauty is physiological. People can do quite a bit with what they've got. Intellect is physiological. These things are primary and are prior, and life is based upon them. Mental illness is physiological. The desire to take drugs all day is physiological, at least in part. It's socialized, it's culturalized, but there's a physical basis to it. So, to deny that there's a physical basis biologically to the very nature of your own state and society is to render yourself in an impossible position.

Contemporary Western leaders believe with Obama that you can have a sort of post-racial civilization. You can have an attenuated society of groups that are partly broken down—particularly around the edges—and that always minimize and deny the strength and self-assertiveness of their own cultures, if you deny the primal ethnicity that lies underneath it. So, everyone can agree just not to differ too much so that there won't be conflict, but that's not a civilization. That's just a group-based society where people paddle along and hope to avoid getting in trouble.

If current trends continue in Britain, Europe and the world, where do you see society 30 to 40 years from now?

Where? Here just in Britain or more generally?

Here in Britain and then more generally.

Well, I've always said that it will be the end point if there is an end point, and that's a debate. I don't necessarily believe life has an end point. It certainly has a start, and it has an end in death. Social death is more difficult to determine. Nevertheless, in 40 years on present trends, if nothing is done at all to reverse things, well, we'll have gone down with a whimper, basically. We will be a tiny proportion, ethnically and racially, of this society. Liberal mores will have taken over to such a degree that large parts of the intermediate social structures such as the family and so on will have completely collapsed, and there will be total and utter atomization, and individuals will sort of be alone and bereft.

I don't think though that it can go much further. I think the liberal curve has stopped and is negotiating its recession. But the point is: can other forces emerge to push it back further? Everyone's managing their own decline. I think liberalism is beginning to manage the nature of its own decline as we speak. The point is what replaces it, and deep down that is a matter in many ways of courage.

A lot of the problems that face us are ethical really. Do people have the courage to do things? Can they step out of their own lives? British people have been very heroic when their establishments order them to be. They find it very difficult to self-start. They find it very difficult to stand out. They find it very difficult to stand alone, particularly when they've caught social disapproval or cultural disapproval or ideological disapproval. There seems to be a great individual heroism in our group, but there seems to be an element of moral timidity and extreme conservatism and conformity, and people are traumatized by liberal ideas and feel that they can't stand against them. It's what political correctness is. It's just a grammar that polices people in their own mind. Most people can't get out of that, and until you break that down other forces won't emerge.

Many people would like to vote for the far Right but are frightened even of voting for it. They fear that in some way they are sullied, or someone will come for them, or they will lose their job, or people they know won't like them, and so on.

Do you think that as the far Right get more votes, more people elected, that they will be able to shift politics more to the radical Right?

Oh yes, there's no doubt about that. It is a process. Cultural dynamic is a form of energy. There was a philosopher 2,500 years ago called Heraclitus who believed everything was based upon forms of fire, as he called it, energy. The Zoroastrian system, an old Aryan system, is partly based upon that sort of principle. The more you push in one direction the more you get. The moderate Left leads to a less moderate Left and leads to an even less moderate Left and pushes it out.

Although you have to will the thing to go on a bit and there are people who want to stick like in a card game with what they've got. But there is a fearsomeness to events, and the truth is that when a very moderate and rather messy populist party, say, of purported extremism bursts through and makes hay and gets big votes everything changes. Everything changes, and everyone starts adapting to it, and people start changing their positions around it, and spaces open up even for potentialities which would be regarded as worse from a liberal point of view.

So, yes, it's a matter of energy. And there will be a few dissentient liberals who believe that perhaps a moderate far-Right party could be acclimatized to represent the dwindling proportion of indigenous persons and maybe negotiate their travel through the present multicultural stage. There are some who begin to think in those terms. They're regarded as back-sliders in the present situation, but that logic leads to other logics, of course.

It's the logic of Sinn Féin. Once they were ruthless terrorists that no one could dare speak to and their voices would be spoken by actors on the radio. But by intermediate stages—it's taken my lifetime—they are now in government, and yet in a sense they haven't got what they wanted even though they do have power of a sort.

And now Ireland is part of the European Union, the Lisbon Treaty is ruling over Ireland, so Sinn Féin have really broken away from Britain and they've ended up with something just as bad. What's your view of the European Union?

Well, it is an old adage in life that people often get the opposite of what they want and no matter how much they strive for the reverse of it.

Yes, the European Union is ... serious and yet a paper tiger, because the European Union is, in my view, an attempt at a very mild, attenuated liberal German domination, but it's a sort of domination that even the Germans themselves are ashamed of having. Germany is the most powerful country on the continent, and power dominates. It's morally effica-cious for them to be the strongest country in Europe, but the Germans are so defeated morally and mentally and so full of self-hatred and funk that the best they can do is this attenu-ated customs union writ large, with its own currency which is really the Deutschmark again.

So, although many UKIP and anti-federalists see the EU as this great tyrannous engine of oppression, I think of it as a weak, bloated bureaucracy that would actually blow over if kicked really hard. It's true that it may morph into something more aggressive if there is a major challenge to liberalism within the nation-states of the union. I think that's true, but I think the EU is a paper tiger.

You know, the German parliament passes a law that their own troops can't fight in Afghanistan. So, they go out to northern Afghanistan, and they're in the north there where there is no Taliban, because they're in the south. And the German warrior tradition is one of the elite warrior tradi-tions of European civilization. Those troops would be excellent troops, of course, if push came to shove. But Germany is basically too morally broken to allow its own men to fight. I think that's the sort of logic of the EU.

They could have chosen Blair, a sassy, mendacious liar and actor as a president of a new Europe. And instead they choose two bureaucrats who are the lowest common denominator of all the inherent countries who no one's ever heard of. So, it's a timidity. The reason that America and the Soviet Union dominated post-war Europe is because Europe was broken by the bloodbath of the 20th century. Morally broken as well. It's not just physical loss, the ethical loss, fear and funk.

So, I don't want the Euro, and I would wish us to leave the European Union, but in some ways the European Union is an attenuated beastie, but it's got a bit of a kick particularly if it reaches into Britain and arrests people for words they've said and things they've written and ideas they've thought and drags them to the continent and put them in prison. But even that is just the working out of the reaction from the Second World War, largely based on fear.

So, leave the EU, but don't be afraid of it, and don't be afraid of the consequences of leaving it either, which are very minor. We would still be in EFTA, we'd still have trade with most of these countries, we'd have to obey some of their laws to trade with them, but most of them are laws that say you shouldn't pay somebody 50 pence an hour, which I agree with up to a point. I just think we ought to pass them. It's none of their business. But it doesn't mean that they're wrong.

So, no, I don't see the European Union the way some Right-wing people do. The *hard* European Union, the one from Mosley's idea, the eagle amidst the circle of stars, that's a different thing. There are many liberals who secretly fear the EU project and believe it's a Trojan horse and that the Right will come to power in Bulgaria, in Italy, and in other countries and enforce its will on the more moderate liberal countries within the EU.

I don't see that, but it's a useful bogey you can use against liberal opinion, because liberals are always afraid; they're always worried; they're always thinking; they're always gestating new notions of worry and anxiety; they're deeply anal retentive, and one of the points of Right-wing politics is to terrify them, to prey upon their minds with the new monstrousness that is coming. This is *Nightmare on Elm Street*, you know. One, two, three, four, five. Because a lot of politics is in the mind, and you can frighten people. I enjoy frightening liberals. I enjoy tormenting them and putting pins in their bottoms and watching them leap up and down and that sort of thing. It's extremely amusing, and one should play upon their fears, which are very grotesque and quite real . . .

Liberals are very afraid of Islam, militant Islam.

Yes, I know.

Are they right to be so?

Yes, they are, actually, because it's illiberalism as a religion. I'm slightly odd, of course, because I don't want the Islamification of Europe or of this country, but I admire Islam. I'm known to be slightly dissentient on these things. They should exist in their part of the world between Morocco and Indonesia. They have their part of the world. They basically have a sixth of the world. They should keep their bloc; they should keep the *ummah*; they should keep their potentialities. It's a different way of being human.

Most Westerners can't even understand a metaphysical objectivism which is so absolute and you've surrendered to the slavery of God's love as the basis of the system. Most Westerners can't even begin to understand what that's about partly because they've drifted into such a degree of secularity, all religious ideas leave them slightly cold in present modernity, post-modernity.

Islam is a very real threat to contemporary liberalism, because they have misunderstood the nature of the multiculturalism they're trying to bring about. One, many of the people who are flooding into the West are less liberal than the people who are here already. Two, many of them don't like quite a bit of what they see in the West, and it's not that they feel sorry for us. They feel that we're a bit weak and hopeless and will be pushed aside.

Islam is a very Right-wing, if you want to use that conception, sort of system of the world. That's why extremist Catholics converted to it after Vatican II. Some Fascists and National Socialists converted to it as well. Because it's *total* and *absolute*.

It's not our way. Our civilization is based upon, in my review, a reverse principle of open-mindedness and reflexiveness and the evidentialism of which Lady Renouf speaks and the Socratic tradition. I see Western civilization as primarily, but not exclusively, Greco-Roman, primarily in the discourse it uses to think about itself. We begin with the view that there are certain absolutes and certain truths, but we are slightly less certain of what they are, and we wish to test them through life, struggle, evidence, and so forth. That doesn't mean that there are no truths. It doesn't mean that there aren't things that stand outside life. What's happened is we've become confused about our own ideas as a civilization, and that's made us autumnal. We're now in danger from other groups because we're hesitant and have lost the convictions which the West has been traditionally based upon.

Islam's not really a threat to us, because it can't conquer the West from inside. This is my view. It can conquer the West from outside, physically through violence, through demographic shift, through militant propagandization. But the West is based upon a contrary civilizational ethic, and therefore it can't conquer in here. If you notice, virtually no indigenous people, apart from radical extremists and outsiders, have any interest in it at all. It doesn't attract Westerners. It doesn't attract the Western mind. Even people who are interested in it for reasons of religious parallelism or perennialism or discourses of that sort, deep down hardly ever convert, and if they do they convert to Sufism, the most open-minded element of it, or they move away very quickly. So, it can't come from the inside. It can only conquer from the outside. But, of course, if people are weak and broken down and somebody's stronger than them they can hold a gun over them. That is true.

You mentioned Islam from the Maghreb to Indonesia and many Western, or so-called Western, politicians have a sort of dual loyalty to a certain country in the Middle East, which used to be called Palestine.

That's right. Yes.

How would you regard the Islamic challenge to this part of the world?

Well, I think on that issue from their point of view, which is not the same as our point of view ... This is the point, you see. You can understand another's position, but you don't share it. Liberalism has thought about these relativities, you see. I feel your pain so much I want to stand in your place. Well, no one would really do that in relation to us. But that's a logical position. I mean, the Islamic condemnation and/or the Arab nationalist and sort of persons of color attitudes towards Israel is completely legitimate, because it's a terrorist state which has seized Palestinian land and held it by force.

It's not totally our problem, but we will always be dragged into it by virtue of the power that group has and manifests in the United States and the fact that Britain is beholden to the United States to such a degree. Michael Portillo virtually said in the 1990s when he was Defence Minister under the Tories, "We have no foreign policy. It's dictated to us by the United States." This means we are drawn *endlessly* into their firefights and their micro-wars and their micro-just-about-to-go-major wars in the Middle East and further afield, all of which, in an attenuated way, are done in order to make that state safe.

However, that state is armed with nuclear weapons and is determined to tough it out and fight it out if there's no other option. So, it's a very difficult proposition, and the trouble is that liberals have made a mess of things. They have mixed everything together. There could be a benign outcome, there could be a middling and confused outcome, and there could be a terrible outcome for many, many people as yet unborn. And we don't really know.

Don't forget, when Obama came to power, the CIA—who got many, many things wrong including weapons of mass destruction in the destroyed country of Iraq, but then again they may have known that these theses were incorrect from the very beginning—told Obama that there would be a nuclear war, that means a nuclear exchange, in the Middle East in the next 25 years. And they don't get everything wrong, because they predicted the war between Georgia and the new Russia under Putin and Medvedev a year before it happened. Now, it's only an intelligence report, and they produce these reports all the time. Russia had a war game recently in which Poland and the Czech Republic were annihilated. So, governments and states do these things all the time. But there is a real civilizational flashpoint there, a tectonic plate flashpoint between the peoples and cultures of the world, and Israel is there forcing, forcing, forcing the flashpoint as a charger.

My view is that the West should decouple from Israel. They have their own destiny. They should do what they want. My view, ultimately, is the view of Islamic radicals in reverse. That they *leave* the West, that they build Islam in the *ummah*. But there's a price to pay there for us and that is that we leave the Middle East, we leave trying to meddle, we leave trying to seize their oil, we leave intervening in their countries, we leave overthrowing groups in their countries that we don't like. It's not our business. We're in a post-imperial world now.

And we throw Israel over, and we say that Israel is not our concern. People will put it in different ways and people will say they're not really anti- but they wish to be neutral and so on, but the consequence is the same. We move back and there's a separation.

Deep down, many Muslims want a separation. They want a world of blocs, because they sort of realize that they might conquer the West in certain demographic terms, although many worry that Muslims will secularize under Western influence. Western ideological power is very severe, and the West is very weak but incredibly highly armed. Bush took down Saddam's regime in 10 days, and it was one of the most ferocious governments in the Third World. Never forget the power the West can unleash. Leaders even like Nick Griffin are not liberals. If they had power they would use it in certain circumstances.

Blair once said that we are going to war in relation to Iraq and these other matters because if we don't, and we don't protect Western societies even in their present constituted-ness, others will come behind us who do not share our values, and they will do it for the masses. He's talking about what he would call non-humanist forms of opinion, by which he means certain well-known political tendencies, about which liberals think all the time. They never stop thinking about these tendencies, because they are their inverse, you see.

Do you think there will be a war with Iran? Israel–Iran? America–Iran?

One doesn't know. It's difficult to predict. There are tendencies both ways. I think if there was going to be a really devastating first strike it would have happened under Bush. Ashkenazi lobbies in the United States never trusted Obama, don't really want it, didn't really want him to be president, wanted Hillary Clinton to be president. She was really their candidate. She promised a devastating attack upon Iran if Israel ever experienced a first strike.

Iran is still quite a way off a nuclear weapon. My understanding is they've hidden their nuclear sites in 56 or 57 places. Many of them are under schools; many of them are under hospitals; many of them are under mountains. My view is that they will probably be able to develop fissionable material for a warhead each year from now on, but Mossad is said to believe they won't be able to weaponize it until at least 2015. That's a window of 5 to 6 years.

One doesn't know. If Israel is to hit them, they will have to refuel in the air. They will not take the risk of their pilots having to bail out across the Middle East where they will be hunted down and killed by whatever Arab country they come down over. America will have to refuel them, which means we'll have to basically allow the strike to take place. Russia has sold Iran a lot of very advanced kit, which they can use to hit the Israelis if they attack them in the air. Iran is basically on the cusp of developing a large number of missiles that can hit all the American bases in Iraq and in Afghanistan. If Iran orders the Shia to rise against the American forces inside Iraq there will be utter chaos, and the Shia are loyal to them, not to anyone else.

Americans have achieved the exact opposite of what they wanted in the Iraqi adventure. They've extended the Shia caliphate from Tehran to the borders of Israel, and that's exactly the reverse of what they wanted. Yet another example of people get the worst of what they want.

What we have to do is try to decouple ourselves from Third World revenges, particularly against this state in the Middle East, that don't really concern us and that we could be dragged down into the welter and tail-end of in a way that's totally counter-propositional and not really in our interests at all.

So, if we decouple ourselves from Israel how will the very influential Jewish minority in Britain . . .

Particularly in the United States. Well, they'll go berserk and they'll start screaming and screaming and screaming. You'll just have to face that screaming down. I believe you adopt the following proposition: that no one is physically harmed, but the West has certain specific interests which are its and with which it *must* align with if it is to survive.

I take the example of the Mel Gibson film.[1] I'm not a Catholic. I'm not a Christian. When Gibson, who is a Hollywood star admittedly, the son of Australia's most controversial man, he's a combination of the Pope and Colin Jordan as was, [sic] produces a film and everyone in American mass media

1 *Passion of the Christ.*

screams and screams and screams for months. And yet it's on at every multiplex, he gets it distributed by Disney affiliates and by Icon Films; it's on every bus shelter kiosk; it's in every WHSmith's; it's on Amazon; it's on the side of billboards. It's now grossed 500 million dollars. It's the ninth most successful film in world cinematographical history.

So, what do we think of that? In the end, he's just stood up to a lobby and stood up to its screaming, and he stood up to its abuse, and he's faced it down. He's still alive and he's made other films, one film anyway, and he's gone on. In a way, you have to sort of take the screaming and fight the cultural war. But many people find it very, very difficult not because they're so frightened that when somebody waves their fist at them they won't do anything. It's a moral fear.

Again, it's to return to what we began with in our little question and answer session here tonight, and that is ethical issues. I think that everything that is wrong with the West isn't structural, isn't socio-economic. These are the epiphenomena and the symptoms of the decline. The decline is inside, and the decline is mental. Only when the mental processes change all the physical outside phenomena can naturally be reorganized. Not easily, it will be very difficult, but when the mentality is different everything else changes. What you see around you is the expression of the mentality, not the reverse.

The real question you always have to ask is why have Westerners got so slothful about their self-regard and why do they believe in ideas which could be sleepwalking towards the near extinction of their kind, their culture, their civilization? No one knows how it will work out, because no one ever does. But why are they so asleep in relation to the processes which are occurring? But the truth is they aren't asleep, because they talk about these things often in a silly and attenuated way all the time.

Someone likened the inherent existence of the Jews as a race to the giant panda as a species. The giant panda is often referred to by naturalists as a species already on the brink of extinction via natural processes and that the giant panda's continued existence may only be attributable to external intervention. Do you agree with this view and, if so, to what extent?

Yes, I haven't had it put like that. Many Jewish leaders, of course, are deeply worried by the processes of assimilation, nice humanism, and integration that are eating into them.

The Jewish census says that 3,000 Jews cease to be Jews in a self-definitional way every year within Britain. Rabbi Jonathan Sacks, who is the leader of that community in a titular way and is a conservative man really, believes that they are being assimilated to the point of semi-destruction, and there's a streak of truth to that.

But of course you cannot proselytize a liberal humanism, particularly from the reform Jewry's perspective, for decades and not expect it to boomerang and come back on you. Many people aren't vanguardists. You know, most people just want an easy life based on commerce and family, and any chance to deconstruct they'll take it. So, if you advocate the deconstruction of groups it will reverberate and come back on you.

No group can escape the logic of part of its own thinking. Particularly, you cannot say in this world, "What I want for others is not what I want for my own group" if you're spreading a universal message. If you're a tribalist, which is philosophically a nominalist, you can talk in specific group-based terms. But not if you want the whole of the rest of the world to be different from the way that you are. You would just join the rest. And the gentilization of many Jews is well underway in Western Europe, so much so that Israel is too much of an identification. Many of them do not want to go fight for that country, do they? They want to stay here in the West.

I have some questions, some of them about the British National Party. Are you happy to answer them? [. . .]

No, it's all right. One should stand and deliver.

Many people in the Conservative Party and UKIP sympathize with many of the BNP's policies, but have a hard time understanding the BNP's economic policies. You may, no doubt, be aware that earlier this year Norman Tebbit referred to the BNP as "Labour with racism."

Yes, yes.

So, which economic policies, if any, mark the BNP out from parties such as Labour and the SWP?[1]

Yes, well, I think the SWP really doesn't exist now as a force that's coherent from the sort of mobocracy of so-called anti-fascism. But in the 1970s the National Front was demonized by the Tory media for middle class people as a socialist

1 Socialist Workers Party.

party with the union flag. When I read *The Telegraph* when I was a teenager it said, "Forget Rhodesia, forget hanging and flogging, forget immigration policies," which they knew instinctively a lot of their readers would sympathize with the National Front about, "concentrate on economics. They're socialist. They will tax you. They believe in socialized medicine, socialized education and so on. They are little different from the center-Left of the Labour Party. Do not go there." And that's slightly convincing to many bourgeois people. Of course, they are only a proportion of the society.

I think the way to approach it is to take a different view, and that is: people are class divided, but it's also divide and rule. Many middle class people are deeply patriotic, often in a rather confused in a populist way, but they are. There are few middle class people who rub their hands with glee at the working class torment during Thatcher's recession in the early 1980s, contrary to propaganda, because most people have an instinctual patriotism.

The way in which you get around all these difficulties, you say to the bourgeois class, "It may be difficult for you in part, but there are large swathes of the population that the Conservative Party never thinks about, never represents, doesn't even *think* about representing and never existed for. They are part of the nation, and you have to have socio-economic vehicles which covers all of that. However, the difference from the socialism of the Left in terms of the sociality of the Right is that the moral premise is different. The Left believes the enforcement of equality through social engineering—as a result of deficit financing and other measures—is good, whereas the Right believes it's either incidental, occasionally necessary, but bad if it leads to undue equality. Inequality is always the goal. Therefore, the Right-wing form of social interventionism is paternal, so the ethic that lies behind it is different."

So, when Tories say you're just a group of socialists waving a flag they're wrong, because the Right doesn't believe in equality in the way that the Left does, and, therefore, all of its socio-economic propositions—that you have a managed capitalism within a nationality, that people who are straight-forwardly successful and entrepreneurial come up to the top, but at the same time they can't suddenly close down a factory and move it to Hungary and then move it to Indonesia and cut all the workers' wages because it's in their interest to do so, because they have a responsibility to the society, to the people that they come from, to the area in which they are born. There's a national development to economic life which superintends my profit, my firm, my life, a sort of purely libertarian attitude.

Deep down, although many businessmen will explode at the hearing of that, many of them secretly agree with those sorts of ideas actually, but never thought you could say so. Because if you do say so you're a "fascist," aren't you? You're one of them. The people we fought in the war, the people who shouldn't be listened to and all that.

Projections indicate that Islam will probably be the largest active religious denomination in the UK by the middle of this century. Do you have a message for British people who are looking for an alternative to the Church of England within which to express their own spiritual feeling?

Yes. I think firstly you've got to think about these matters. Religions are largely about death and about facing it. In other words, it's about the meaning of life, which ends in death. So, white people have got to free themselves from the telly and *The X-Factor* and premier league football and other inanities. And many of them do, because they all have lives; they all have tragedies; they all have dilemmas. We certainly are in a philosophically vapid phase because we've privatized our belief systems, and we've said that people can believe in it in your own home, in your own skull, but there's no social and cultural ramification.

Rowan Williams is in Rome at the moment and does not speak for England. And I'm not talking here about some silly point about the fact that he's partly Welsh. He doesn't speak for anyone other than his own attenuated bureaucracy. That's also partly the fault of the English and British. These high important problems with which these systems deal are important.

I believe that people can be as Christian as they want culturally, but they should be ethically pagan. They should look at the Greco-Roman and Nordic world. They should learn more about their history, culture, and civilization. They should be less dualist. They should adopt stronger and more articulate formulations that will mentally toughen them up a little bit. All of these things are available. The philosophers who advocate many of these things, Schopenhauer (a little bit), Kierkegaard (yes and no), Nietzsche (very much), they're all in Waterstones. They're not secret. They're not banned. They're not hidden away. If you want it you can go and find it, but it's got to exist in you first.

Given the way in which neo-conservative and Israeli policies have exacerbated social polarization of the West to the point where the inherent structural weaknesses of a multi-racial society have been arguably exposed sooner than they would have otherwise, would it not, in a perverse way, be correct in saying such policies are helpful to the rise of the radical Right in Europe?

Yes, I think that's true. But liberalism's based upon a false view. It's partly based upon the Pelagian heresy within Christianity that man is naturally good, when man is not. Go to any liberal history book in a modern library and get it out for a half an hour, and you will realize that human beings have more than an unpleasant side. So, the belief that enormous numbers of people can come from all over the world and can mix together happily because we are all really the same—and there are human criteria, we all are human—but there are important perspectival and situational and experiential and even physical differences which lead people to perceive the world differently and want different things. Many people do just want a quiet life, but their vanguards that give them the identity in the first place, will inevitably tend into conflict because they want to maximize the strength of their own partial way of seeing things.

The idea that you can be on everyone's side and yet be yourself simultaneously isn't true. You can *understand* many other positions. That is true. And the irony is that many liberal humanists don't really like the people that they protest to adore, because they all want them to become Westerners. They want them to lose their identity, and they want the West to merge in with them, and there are subtle forms of "racism" and "racialism" in the liberal agenda that every African can become British. What about his own identity? What about his own tribal identity, which is for them the national identity, the primary biological sense of belonging? What does it mean to be a Vambo or to be Kraa if you're just stuffed into some state in South London? The idea that they adore these people and they want only the best for them isn't really true.

There's also the patriotism of the immigrants themselves. If I was born in another group I would want to be in my own country and do something for that and build that up and see that that achieves something more. So, the finger can be pointed at all these people who see rich pickings in the West and just want to come in.

But yes, liberalism is speeding up the process, because its view of human nature is wrong. Human nature has a loving and sympathetic side, but it also has an avaricious and competitive and aggressive side, and they have not computed that properly.

To what extent do you agree with this statement: "If you change a people, you change the culture, which in time will change their laws and the ethics that govern that culture."

Yes, I think that's a factual statement, and this means that contrary to what many conservatives believe, that it's all a bit of an accident what's going on now—there is a deliberative and intentional element to it. Many liberals do not see it in those terms and do not view the world in those terms. I'm slightly paradoxical, of course, because most Right-wing people are very prone to seeing the world in those terms, because I am a Nietzschean, and I slightly view the world in a more dynamic sort of way, a more energy-based way.

But there is a logic to the processes ongoing even in their semi-chaos, and liberalism is a chaotic system. But there's only so much dissonance that any ideology can meaningfully contain. I think we're reaching the point of maximum stretch now. The assimilation into Western modernity of groups which are totally non-Western and completely pre-modern is causing enormous tension to the degree that the whole project faces a degree of even moral collapse.

Slightly similar question: In an interview, Nick Griffin stated that the Labour government's own projections [predict] a white ethnic minority Britain by the year 2100. Do you agree with this statement and, if so, why?

I think it is largely true, because people will move in and out. Things always take longer. The Tories will come in. Tories manage the decline better. Major allowed 100,000 migrants in. Labour 300,000 per year, plus illegals. Labour always radicalizes the process of dissolution, and partly wishes to, and partly is in a confused state and can't really govern properly, and partly is pushed by the *modus operandi* of their own ideas. So yes, I think that's actually a totally factual statement. Contrary to the idea that's spread by Jack Straw and others that people like Griffin are always scaremongering and shouting the odds, that sounds a completely rational and even cautious statement to my mind.

In what sense do you understand men and women to be different, and in what ways should societal and other institutional discrimination reflect those differences?

I think life determines the difference. I think it is biological. Males and females have different brains, therefore wish to socialize and interact, even with each other, in completely different ways. Deep down, almost everyone understands that.

There's always a problem with the proportion of women who are completely capable of doing quite advanced male careers. Do you rip up what society always was in order to facilitate this active, energetic, gifted, and militant minority to get their own way? The West has decided to do that. It's made an enormous number of other people rather unhappy, both male and female: 70% of women just want a home-based option, a man and children, despite all the ideology that goes around, but there's still 30% that would want something different.

The Western tradition is slightly different to the Asiatic, the Negroid, the Arab, the Eurasian, and others. Women have always had more of a stake publicly in Western societies. In Germanic societies, the women often fought behind the men, but the men went first.

I am opposed to feminism. But at the same time there are very gifted women who can do certain public roles. But as long as you ideologize on behalf of what deep down most men and women want, the truth is that natural biology will take care of these things. You have to apply immense pressure on the society to get it to act in a counter-propositional and non-biological way. So, you have to engage in intense propagandistic efforts through media to try to reverse gender roles and enforce sort of inverted stereotypes on people.

If you take all of that off and allow the natural "political incorrectness" of gender roles to proliferate you'll find that you'll have the odd MI5 chief who's a woman; you'll have the odd judge who's a woman. But broadly speaking you'll have a sort of traditional society where the roles are quite clearly male and female. And deep down no woman respects a man who doesn't think that, although they don't like him saying it.

In what ways do you think that the differences between resistance to cultural and political Marxism in the United States and Canada and resistance to cultural and political Marxism in Europe will manifest themselves over the course of the remainder of this century?

That's an interesting one. I think in a strange way they'll take the same form whether the societies are in quite different stages of development. America's different. America's in a more radical state. It's further into decline, but there's bigger space. There's more chance of a sort of moral Rightist resurgence there. There's a lot of energy there. Europe's quite tired, I think, and needs to wake up quite quickly, but can.

Yes, that's an interesting one. I think the great difficulty in America is a third political force. If things emerge in America it will be ideological. Many of the various Right-wing books of the 20th century in English have been written by Americans. People like Revilo P. Oliver, Francis Parker Yockey, Lawrence R. Brown. They've contributed quite a lot, and yet their movements have almost been completely marginal. But then just by adopting a coherent form of thinking you can actually change reality quite a bit. But White people essentially come from Europe and their destiny deep down is in Europe, and therefore Europe is ultimately more important.

I think the intellectual tradition here is richer and stronger and the political tradition against liberalism in some ways is even more robust. So, I think some of the ideas that a successful break out in Europe may use will come from America, but I think America's destiny is in Americans' hands. I think the greatest thing America can do is to foster neo-isolationism in the middle and end of the 21st century. If America turns back on itself the rest of the world will be liberated from its thrall and there is a prospect for a European rebirth.

I once heard you say that if Adolf Hitler's Germany had not had the second Allied front to contend with the Third Reich and its Axis allies would have surely rolled up and obliterated the Soviet Union. Yet it is difficult for some people to accept this, since the Allies did not land in Sicily and Normandy until the middle of 1944 and by the time they did the German army had already suffered catastrophic defeats at Stalingrad, at Kharkov, at Smolensk, at Kursk, et al. and were on the general defense in Russia. Is there any additional information that you could possibly bring to light in order to persuade such persons otherwise?

Not really of a technical sort. I think it's just that the Germans came this close to winning the Second World War as everyone knows. That's why this period is still not integrated into normal history. It's not a normal event because they came so close to winning. The subtext to the ferocity of retrospective opposition even when in a sense it's slightly unreal, Hollywoodized, and doesn't really matter, is because they came so close. The margin of winning in a battle is often very thin.

I personally think if there was no Western front and no Western threat and America had stayed out of the conflict with any European connection whatsoever and Britain was neutral and maybe Churchill wasn't Premier (and all of these things are enormous ifs) you would have had an enormous fight between the Germans and the Soviets. And if they had been less distracted, if they had pursued more radically the desire of getting to Moscow and forcing regime change, and maybe forcing nationalistic Russian generals to oust the communists, as could have occurred in a certain set of circumstances, if they had knocked out one of the major Russian cities. Those are big ifs.

If they'd not gone down into the Ukraine, if Italy hadn't sort of engaged in *cul-de-sac* type activity down in the Balkans and drawn German troops in . . . there's just a chance. They had one chance to knock Russia out. Once that chance went they would lose the war. Germany's not strong enough. It's enormously powerful, but it's not strong enough to dominate the whole of Eurasia unless it goes for a knock-out blow and it's instantaneously successful in a sort of Alexander the Great way. Once that chance was missed they would lose, although they could have perhaps had an attritional war that would have gone on for decades, you know, as the Soviets moved further West and they frustrated them all they could.

But they had to knock out Russia quick and early and they didn't. Russia is immensely powerful and a very difficult country to defeat.

Can we take a break? Are you tired?

I'm all right. Nietzscheans believe in struggle and going on to the end.

How crucial is the failure in the economy to the rise of viable mainstream alternatives to Western liberal democratic capitalism?

That's a complicated one. I mean, economy is all that matters to people because they've been told that it is. The Muslims are right on the Western obsession with the right to shop at least from that point of view. People are materialistic, they've been raised to it, religion has receded into the background, artistic matters are regarded as a form of entertainment or, at best, peripheral. Therefore, if people are hurt in their pocket they start screaming and they want vengeance against the system and they will vote for radical people. It's not a brilliant scenario, but it's the fact.

It is probably true that the amount of debt that we are all swimming on, everyone in this room is £55,000 in debt whether they like it or not, that is the basis of all the debts that have been run up. If that comes crashing down upon people, people will react, and people are sort of aware that there is one party out there that people, particularly indigenous people and others as well in this confused welter of sort of semiotic and reverse semiotic, could well react.

So, yes, for most people these economic things are crucial. Once they are hit and sustain damage, the most moderate person can become red in tooth and claw. I would prefer if people change their ideas, but people won't, and therefore they need the pressure of material circumstances to do that, and that takes an economic form.

What, if anything, should people realize when they turn on their TV screens only to see a female and/or ethnic minority newsreader more than 50% of the time?

That it's deliberate. That it's a human form of product placement. It's basically saying that the liberal changes which have occurred demographically and sexologically in terms of the cultural revolution from the 1960s are irreversible. You can moan all you like. There is nothing to be done. These changes are irreversible. So, every time they turn the TV on, it's ideology.

If they turn the internet on, and I believe digital TV will soon have these things where you have a small web in the corner and you can go click it into it so you can use the TV to access the internet in other words, and I would imagine that almost every digital set after the switch over from analog will have that.

So, my hope is (1) that they realize it's all propaganda, (2) they realize that the internet enables them to choose the propaganda they want, and (3) they use the internet to look at alternative viewpoints about the same matters.

Ultimately, it's not who reads the news, it's what lies behind what's on the screen and not how it's written and presented by any spokesman or whatever, but the ideas that lie behind it. Ideas rule the world, in my view. But the reason why those newscasters are as you describe is because of an alternative set of ideas that has triumphed.

You have often described yourself as a pagan. As you will no doubt be aware, there are many people today who also describe themselves as pagans. Indeed, I myself once joined the official pagan society at my university only to discover that it was in fact dominated by people who bore an astonishing resemblance to the Flower Power Hippie movement of the 1960s and 1970s. [. . .] Could you just briefly explain what sort of paganism it is that you represent and how, if at all, it is distinguished from other so-called pagan movements such as Wicca?

Yes, that's a very good question, and it's essentially truthful, because most people know in their hearts that those who describe themselves as pagans are prone to be like that. That university experience is likely to be a little "extreme," but broadly speaking it's morally true as an essay in discovery.

My view is quite simple. Paganism and Christianity are the wrong way around. Christianity has influenced our culture for 2,000 years. Christianity has provided the ethical and aesthetic superstructures through which most Western people think. Reality is pagan. Man is pagan. Nature is pagan. Pagans have reacted against Christianity—which is deep down a "Left-wing" religion of humanism, love, and tolerance—in an aggressive, Leftist, and alternative way. Contemporary pagans believe that Christians are conservative, that they're stuffy, that they stand for *Daily Mail* and family-concentric values. They will rebel against that in every respect. And Christians think of pagans as woolly, alternative Leftists who want to tear things down.

In actual fact, paganism is pre-Christian, is barbaric, is natural law oriented, is morally fascistic. However, pagans would scream and scream and scream at the idea of that and would run from the room. Christianity is a religion of tolerance, love, and peace. So, they're the wrong way around. They're completely the wrong way around.

In their false symmetry or asymmetry, they indicate everything that's happened. It's part of the generalized tragedy, you know. A lot of Christian people are those that remain a bit residually patriotic, quite Right-wing, and a lot of pagans are beyond *The Guardian*. The two are the wrong way around.

I'm not anti-Christian in the sense of culturally disavowing it, because you cut off 70% of the way in which the West achieves what it is. It can't be done and shouldn't be attempted, in my view. The change is ethical. Everyone's a pagan really. Somebody pushes you, you push them back.

The Catholic school I went to had a lovely little chap who taught piano and he said to me, "Why is there so much bullying in this school?" He said, "This is a Catholic school. This is a Christian school. Every day I go in, and the boys are bullying each other. I saw a boy with his blazer over his head and another boy was booting him. Booting him in the playground!" He was quite morally shocked. He was genuinely morally a Christian man, which very few people are, and I respected him for that, because it is a conceptual and an ethical and a spiritual viewpoint. Hardly any Christians are really like that. It's a cultural label that they've adopted, that I was born into, that everyone in the West was born into at one time or another.

I said to him, "Because human nature's like the way that they are. It's an all-male school. They're fighting violently amongst each other for hierarchy and supremacy, and it's a test." He said, "But that's terrible! That's horrible! That means that we're not that much beyond a gorilla colony." And I said, "That's life. You have an ideal about how it should be, but it's not how it is."

And so these pagans are worse than a travesty really, you know. It is ridiculous. Although some of their truth that good and evil go together, that reality is non-dualist, that nature dominates life, that nature has a sacred dimension, those are actually true. But essentially you've got the leavings and the cultural spastics and that sort of thing all gathered together in one area, whereas paganism is really about strength and morality and growing towards the sun. And you don't have to believe in gods and goddesses. They're just a personification of those forces.

When did you decide to convert to paganism and why?

Well, I never really converted to paganism. I mean, there are some orthodox pagans, if you can have such a thing, who probably think I am not one. But I'm a Nietzschean and that's a different system. Somebody made this for me. [Points to odal rune pendant.] And I like Odinic paganism sort of as an objectification of my sort of sensibility. Does one believe the gods objectively exist in another realm? Well, you see, religion is a philosophy about life which is sacristic and has rituals in which you partly act out, therefore it's more important because it's made slightly more concrete than ideas or it's really just based upon ideas. There are relatively simple but powerful ideas at the crux of all the big religious systems. Most people are born in a system and just accept that and go along with it as long as it's not too onerous or they feel like they live their life through it properly.

I just agree with the ethics of that type of Nordic paganism, which is really how the Vikings lived and how they behaved. I'm less concerned with small groups, which I respect. I like the Odinic Rite, but I personally believe that those sorts of things will only ever activate post-modern minorities and very small ones at that.

I think people should identify with what they think they are and the values that they hold. This symbol really means strength or courage or masculinity or the first man or the first principle of war or the metaphysics of conflict. So, I just think it's a positive system of value.

I never really was a Christian. Culturally, I have great admiration for elements of Christian art. More so than most people who are pagan who have violently reacted against it. I don't really share that emotionalism. But I don't agree with Christian ethics. Deep down, they've ruined the West, and we're in the state that we are because of them.

Just added on to that: How do we create more Nietzscheans? How do we spread Nietzscheanism as a religion, as an idea?

You've got to get people quite young. I think you've got to introduce alternative value systems to them. This is a society that says weakness is good, weakness should be pitied, the ill are weak, the disabled are weak, people who've got various things wrong with them (too fat, too thin, bits dropping off) they need help. They *may* need help. But the value system that lies behind that desire to help worships the fact of weakness and the fact that people are broken. If you worship the idea of strength and tell the weak to become stronger, which is a reverse idea for helping them essentially. You help them in order to get stronger. You totally reverse the energy pattern and you've reversed the system of morals that exists in this culture now. You've reversed the sort of things that Rowan Williams or his predecessor or his likely successor always says, basically. I think that's what you have to do.

I personally think it's a moral revolution, not anything political, that will save the West, because all the technology is here, all the systems of power are here. You only have to change what's in people's minds. It's very difficult though.

So, to a young person watching this video, never heard of you before, where would he go to find out about Nietzscheanism?

Just go to the Wikipedia page, surprisingly, although it's a bit trivial, is actually quite accurate in a tendentious way. Although some of the philosophical debates about him and the genealogy of his works might confuse people because it views it in an academic way. And you don't need to put his name to it. There's a cluster of power-moral, individualistic, elitist, partly antinomian, partly gnostic, partly not, partly pagan, vitalist and other ideas which go with that sort of area.

Strength is morality. Weakness is sin. Weakness requires punishment. If you're weak, if you're obese, if you're a drug addict, become less so. Become stronger. Move towards the sun. Become more coherent. Become more articulate. Cast more of a shadow. It's almost a type of positive behaviorism in some ways. But it's not somebody wagging their finger and so on, because you're doing it for yourself. It comes from inside.

Do you not think though that Nietzscheanism doesn't have a transcendental element to it?

That's why I'm wearing this [rune pendant], you see, because I probably think there ought to be such a thing. Many people need to go beyond that. If his thinking before he went mad, probably because he had tertiary syphilis, it's up to sort of 1880, so we're talking about thinking that's 130 years old.

I think in some ways he's an anatomist of Christianity's decline, because Christianity been declining mentally and in some ways extending out into the Third World where it's real catchment area now is. I mean, there will be a non-White pope soon. Christianity will begin to wear the face of the south very soon. It's the ideal religion for the south. It's pity for those who fail, for those who are weak, for those who are hungry, for those who are broken. Have pity on your children, O Lord. It's an ideal religion. Don't take it through violence or fear or aggression. Submit and be thankful for what He will give you in His wisdom.

But it's ruining us. For centuries we were strong even despite that faith, but of course we made use of it. The part that fits us is the extreme transcendence of Christian doctrine. That's what Indo-Europeans like about that faith. The enormous vaulting cathedrals, the Gothic idea that you can go up and up and up. It's that element in it that we like, and we made into ourselves. But we forgot the ethical substratum. We forgot the sort of troll-like ethical element that there is no other value but sympathy, there is no other value than compassion, that love is the basis of all life. And ultimately that is a feminine view of civilization which will lead to its collapse in masculine terms.

How would you view the works of Julius Evola?

Yes, they're the counter-balance to Nietzsche. There is a lot of religious elements in there of a perennialist sort that a lot of modern minds can't accept. You see, Nietzsche is a switchblade, and nearly all people in this society are modern even if they think they're not. Nietzsche is a modern thinker. Nietzsche is a modernist. Nietzsche can reach the modern mind. Nietzsche's the most Right-wing formulation within the modern mind that people can accept.

My view is that people who accept Evola straight out aren't living in the modern world. That's not a criticism. It's a description of where they are. I think for people to become illiberal they have to become illiberal first within the modern world. Some people would say you have to go outside of it. You know, the culture of the ruins and the revolt against the modern world, *per se*. But I personally think that we're in modernity.

But there will be people who go to Nietzsche and *Thus Spake Zarathustra*, which is really a semi- or pseudo-religious text, is not enough and they'll want to go beyond that and they'll want a degree and a tier of religiosity. The dilemma always in the West is what to choose. Back to Christianity or on to paganism? Which system do you choose?

Evola said he was a Catholic pagan, didn't he? One knows what he means. But I see paganism peeping out of everything. I see paganism peeping out of Protestantism, the most Jewish form of Christianity, through its power-individualism and its extremist individuality (Kierkegaard, Carlyle, Nietzsche). I see paganism saturating Catholicism and peeping out of it at every turn, aesthetically, artistically, the art of the

Renaissance, the return of the Greco-Roman sensibility, the humanism of the ancient world. Some of the greatest classicists were Medieval Popes and so on. I see it just looming out. The whole structure of the Catholic Church is a Roman imperial structure, Christianized. So, I see it peeping out.

Our law is Roman. All of our leaders were educated and steeped in the classical world to provide a dialectical corollary to Christianity without them being told that's what is happening. The decline of the classics is partly because people don't want to go back there, basically. So, you don't teach it to anyone apart from tiny little public school elites, which are 0.2% of the population who read a few authors who no one else even knows exist. You know, big deal.

The difficulty with Evola is that it's a very great leap for the modern mind. Although in his sensibility, I agree with his sensibility, really. I agree with him going out amidst the bombings, not caring. I agree with that sort of attitude towards life, which is an aristocratic attitude towards life. But we're living in a junk food, liberal, low middle class society. You've got to start where you are. I think Nietzsche is strong enough meat for most people and is far, far, far too strong for 80% now.

Today, the mentally disabled have been allowed into the Paralympics. So, you will have the 100 yard cerebral palsy dash at the next Olympics in London in 2012. This is the world we're living in. Nietzsche would say that's ridiculous and so on. And that is a shocking and transgressive and morally ugly attitude from the contemporary news that we see. So, it's almost as if Nietzsche's tough enough for this moment.

But I'm [interested] in that he said, "God is dead in the minds of men." That doesn't necessarily mean, of course, although he was a militant atheist, he's living open the idea that . . . [God objectively exists—Ed.]. You see, the Christian idea of God was dying around him, mentally, and it has died. I mean, hardly anyone really, deep down, believes that now. Even the people who say that they do don't in the way that they did 100 years ago or their predecessors did.

So, it has died, but I think there are metaphysically objectivist standards outside life. Whether our civilization can revive without a return to them is very open. It's very questionable. Where that discourse is to come from is . . . The tragedy would be if Christianity sort of facilitated our greatness, but ended up ruining us, which of course might be the true thesis.

Now we're getting into deep waters.

What is your view of Abrahamic religions?

I think religion is a good thing. The Right always supports the right of religion to exist. Religion does cross ethnic and racial boundaries. Afghanistan was Buddhist once. I prefer people to have some sort of religious viewpoint, even the most tepid sort of thing, [than] none at all, because at least there is a structure that is in some sense prior.

But, personally, I prefer tribally based religions. I prefer religions that are about blood and genetics and honor and identity and are nominalist and that are specific. But I think people will adopt different systems because they're physiologically different even within their group. You can see that about certain people. Certain people, Christianity suits them very well and they can be quite patriotic and quite decent people and so on in that system and there we are. But for me? No.

I'm a barbarian in some ways. People can worship what gods they want within the Western tradition, and that's all right.

[...]

I never write my speech till I stand up.

How do you do that? Give us some sort of idea.

I do. But I like performance. It's not an effort for me. Although today tired me. Today I was sort of performing, you know, in the performance. It was a sort of performance in the performance. It was a bit *ugh*. But I like doing it, you know. I don't have to do it. I'm not one of these pathetic performers. Actors and performers are two types. They're sadist or masochists, really, and I'm a sadist, you see? Whereas most performers are masochists. They're on pills, everyone must love them, if they have a "boo" in the audience they're prostrated for a day, and all this sort of thing. They reinvent themselves each time they go before the camera. Whereas the other polarity is Orson Welles: an egomaniac who believes the world must look at him and so on, and I'm like that. [laughs]

Do you actually start off with something in your head and then you build on from that?

No. Well, I know I'm going to talk about Punch and Judy, but otherwise I don't really know. I know some of the skits. Jewish comedians would call it *shtick*. The sort of stuff you come out with. Because there are routines. Punch is on the ground, the crocodile's eating him, and the doctor comes up. I know those routines, and I'll fit them in somewhere. But no, I don't know what I'm going to do.

You just get up and do it.

I just get up and do it. But I like doing it, you see. It's natural for me to do it. Whereas most people, they would literally be . . . They talk, "Oh, he's nothing. I could do it." They get up there, and they'd be utterly terrified. I've seen BNP organizers, great hulking blokes who'd take you apart . . .

I remember an Essex meeting, some bikers meeting, and everyone's chanting and you know. I sometimes think, you know, my father's a very posh bank manager, and I'm here in this meeting. I've spoken in some utter dens, pits. I spoke in one place in Burnley with barbed wire all over the meeting. I said to the organizer, "Why's there so much barbed wire over the meeting place?" He said, "It's to keep the scum out!" But he didn't tell me which part of the population he was referring to. Shutters on the windows, you know. There was one shebeen of a place in south London, Merton or something, I spoke at. Good Lord! It was sort of "Yeah, he's right!!!" You know, some bloke would get up and say, "You know what I mean, all right?" And the other bloke would say, "I don't agree with that, mate! I think you need sortin' out!" And they'd almost be fighting in the middle of the meeting. The organizer would go down and sort of kick them like a dog. He actually dragged one bloke out. Hitched him up. You'd better turn this off, actually. Hitched him up and threw him out the meeting saying, "Get out! You're gettin' out, boy!" It's a beer cellar, you know. Sort of semi-uncontrollable.

And yet you do have a power over them. They listen to you. It's interesting, because, you know, there's a few heavies there like Steve and so on, but they have a sort of admiration for you in a way, because they want you to say what they can't. That's what it boils down to.

The vocabulary . . .

Yes, and they admire you for it as well. There's also a class love/hate relationship as well, because a part of them doesn't like you and a part of them adores you. The one vies with the other.

But then patriotism is the only socialism, really, because it holds people together in their difference, because people are different. Did you see that statistic that lower, lower white working class boys now are under-performing every other ethnic group in the society? These are C3s. Homework is a word they don't even know the meaning of.

Yes, when they asked that question on Question Time, they didn't address it at all. They just swept it under the carpet. They said "Education as a whole is failing." When it's black . . . "Oh, they're failing."

Yes, it's racist. Well, they say racist structures from the past, patriarchy, and post-imperial ideas, these people are dumbed down and so on.

I think what's happening with the lower whites is they are literally sort of dying mentally, you know, giving up. All these other groups have come in. A proportion of the Asians that have come in are not stupid at all, some of them are Baboo-like, but they're not stupid, some of them, in a bourgeois way.

There's a hierarchy of working class, of upper middle class . . .

Yes, they've just left the bottom there. Caucasians are, I think, a radical group. So, there's a sort of soaring towards the stars, but there's also a down in the ditch. And I think there are some who decide, "F— it! I'll go right down into the pit. See if I care!" To reach very high-grade activity . . . 90% of the most elite books in the British Library are all written by our group, even though it is a Western-concentric library and all the rest of it. But still if that wasn't true it wouldn't be true even in a Eurocentric context. And yet, at the same time, if you can't reach that, and your status and credibility is tied up with being white, and now in a mixed group society that's no longer true, a proportion of the bottom will just go down and down and down. "Why should I read a book? Why should I do anything!? F— the lot!" And off the cliff. I think a proportion right at the bottom are doing that. A lot of the people above them don't care, because they've written these people off. They don't care about them at all.

I've worked in these pupil referral units for these kids who've just fucked off school, basically. I find some of them are very intelligent because they know how to play the system. They know that if you go to the PRU and wear your track suit all day they only have to do a half-day of school, get outings to reward them for misbehavior. I find them quite intelligent. It's almost like they've seen the system for what it is and say, "Yeah, I'm just going to drop out."

There are a lot of White lads who are doing that.

I'm 47-and-a-half. What will life be like for them when they're 47-and-a-half?

What will life be like for any 16 year old when they're 47-and-a-half?

Ha! Don't say that!

I think they're asking that question now and have decided. They're rejecting the system, because they've seen it's rejected them and they're kinda jumping for the push, the lot of them. I was quite surprised. I've talked to some of these lads. Very intelligent guys, you know. They often put their intelligence to criminal purposes.

Yes. Of course. The only industry left.

Yeah. People feel they're the scum, but they're not. They're intelligent people who use their intelligence in different ways, but they've seen what's happened to the system. I think they could be very useful to us.

Yes, liberals are worried about that group, because they wonder who they might vote for if they ever got the gander to vote, to "engage." Because they would be very radical types indeed.

Well, they certainly don't mind saying what they think about certain things. They actually just don't care about social approval. They say it like it is and they're quite tough lads a lot of them. I'm talking about when I was working in Salford, which is quite a white working class area. Certainly some of their views wouldn't be out of place in a meeting like this, except they'll express them differently.

Yes. The last time I was in Salford I went to the Lowry Museum, which is very interesting, isn't it? Very interesting, because it's an attempt to redeem these post-industrial areas. It looks like something on Canary Wharf, basically. You go in there and it's this Barbican Center in the middle of Manchester. I know there's great tension between Salford and Manchester.

My mother was from Moston. We lived in Manchester when I was 19. So, there's a northern streak to me. I'm very direct for a southerner. I come straight out with it, which is slightly odd. And maybe it's my mother, because my mother had two personalities. People would ring up, and she'd say, "Dorothy Bowden. Henley, 4132." And then she'd say, "Get up! Get down here now!" "Dorothy Bowden, 4162." So, she had these two sort of personalities.

But yes, Lowry is very interesting because he's a very interesting artist. I know he's been made into a cult and so on, but the pictures of distance, the pictures are misanthropic, the pictures see the people in the streets almost like ants.

Well, he's dehumanized them by the way he just literally gets them down to their essence. They're matchstick men, basically.

They're dehumanized. Yes. These incredible pictures of Trade Union and other marches in Manchester and in Salford in the 1930s, and there's no heroic element at all. It's sad, whey-faced types who are for the rubbish heap, marching before they get there. Lowry's been made a humanist cult that he's celebrating Northern grit, that he's celebrating human resistance to the ugliness of industrialization. Bollocks really. If you look at it, it looks like a man who's seeing what's in front of him.

Yes, he tells it like it is, I think.

That's what art is, you see. It's closer to, not science, but it's closer to objectivism than people think. That's what he saw; that's what he painted. It wasn't pleasant, and when he did it everybody hated them.

Sort of like an avant-garde social realism.

That's exactly right. That's very good! That's exactly right, yes. That's exactly what it is. And you see these twits going around saying, "Oh, it's so marvelous! His esteem for the Mancunian poor!" And the Mancunian poor are presented like beetles, basically, amidst these towers. There's an amazing picture where they're going into that football match, into the Latics, into Bolden. That's an amazing picture.

It's funny because these BNP activists dropped me out there, because this is that artsy fuddy-duddy stuff that he likes. He can go and see it. This is their attitude. It's quite funny, actually. I came out, and they said, "What did you think of it then. We think Lowry's really awful!" And I said I really liked it and I could see them going, "Uhh, yeah . . ." But I liked it in a different way, because it was so interesting. And you couldn't give them away. You couldn't *give* them away!

Do you know where Platt Fields is? Yes, we used to live there. We used to live in St. Ives Road which was next to Fallowfield down from Maine Road where Manchester City used to be.

Oh God, what a toilet that was! It was an utter tip even then. We were there in 1981-82. I don't think I'm that soft a Southerner, but when the first time I came there . . . You saw scenes of poverty you'd never see in the South, never seen in my entire life. I thought to myself, "Christ." I saw one bloke. Do you remember those expressionist communist paintings by people like Grosz and so on from the 1920s of veterans who had been wounded in war and on boards with no limbs with wheels on the bottom and that sort of thing? I saw a bloke in Gorton like that in 1980. I thought to myself, "Bloody hell! This is 1980! The Boer War ended in 1902, and there's this bloke like that!" I thought, "Dear, dear, dear." I've never seen poverty like that except in certain pockets in the East End in Old Brick Lane and that sort of thing.

I saw a chap on crutches once in Brick Lane market with no legs. No legs but crutches. You know, the NHS has provided false limbs since 1948, but either he didn't know, or he couldn't get through bureaucracy, or he hadn't been. It was Dickensian. It was straight out of Dickens.

Well, then there's places like Miles Platting.

Oh, Miles Platting. I know Miles Platting very well, yes. It's beaten down to a point that it doesn't exist. It's unbelievable. All of this is part of the inner reason why "I'm not a Tory." Do you see what I mean? I saw this very early in my life.

It's got worse now. It's become extended. If you go down from almost the center, because if you drive from the center of Miles Platting the other way up towards the center, by the time you get to the center you're in Piccadilly. You're right in the center. Miles Platting goes for miles of just boarded up, devastated, post-industrial dereliction. And they've got this zone policy, haven't they, because they're trying to get everybody out to redevelop the city. Trendy Manchester, and the BBC is moving north, and they're forcing all the stars to go up to the studios. Because there used to be a big studio on the Oxford Road, wasn't there?

And you get this sort of Atlanta type feel. You've got a billionaire living in his flat on the top of this block, and he looks down through devastation to some heroin addict injecting on a bed at the bottom, and it's all part of the funky scene, you know? It adds to the *frisson*. For the bloke who's living in the flat!

There's not as much of a social divide is there? That's the thing. It's the social divide. I think people are more economically within the same . . .

Well, the divide is New Labour sort of post-modern elite against the rest. Because there are no Tories in Manchester. They don't exist. They're a species that ceased to exist.

Until you're out in Stretford.

Yes. You have to go right out on the edge. Well, the middle class went to Cheshire, didn't it? To escape. That's where they went.

Because when we lived in Manchester in the early '80s the whole sewer system in the city was Victorian. I mean, Manchester was a great Victorian city, one of the greatest, and that all collapsed in the early '80s. The dignity of the city, because there was no money to pay for anything, just went straight down the toilet. And just up the road Liverpool was taken over by a Trotskyist group in the same era. This is what happened to our great cities.

Because the Tories aren't concerned about those cities, basically, at all. All they're concerned about is the zone in the middle of England and the south, east and west, and around London. And they can form a government with that. So, they've written off these areas in the north. A swathe in the northwest, northeast, central north, much of Yorkshire, the northern part of the East and West Midlands, as far as they're concerned they don't really exist.

Labour just managed them in their decline, and most of their social engineering is destructive. To get people out of Miles Platting they've flooded the whole area with Somalians.

And these great blocks, you know they'll sell to somebody. This block of derelict flats, ex-council flats, legacy of Wilson's planning and all that, they often sell them for 10 pounds. 10 pounds to a developer. Because there's endless deals going on.

Wasn't there that alternative comedian Mel Smith? There was a program in the 1980s called *Muck and Brass* and a lot of Mancunian type politics. It's just like that. "What can I do for you?" "Well, I'll have a think."

I remember a sort of Masonic, this pride culture. I remember I once watched the mayor of Manchester enter the university on the Oxford Road. He was like a Prescott type. He came with his seal of office and the fat wife. "Oh, it's so posh, isn't it?" And they came out of this big car, and they loved it. You could just see it. It's that culture of Labour sort of municipalism in action, and he's some Trade Union bloke. This is his favor at the end of his slog. You know, all those boring committees he sat on. This is the moment when they cash in. Credibility wise.

The moment for me was in 1980 we walked up the Oxford Road. It's very big. It's the central road that goes through the academic area of Manchester University, Polytechnic, Eye College, Art College, further education college, and so on. I saw these two Third World groups demonstrating against each other. The Iranian Revolution had just happened, and all the ones who were pro were marching up and down with pictures of Khomeini, and all the ones who were mujahideen, were a Left-wing group, were anti. They were all marching up and down showing pictures of blokes being tortured and all this.

I could see the GMP, the Greater Manchester Police. James Anderton, that Protestant fundamentalist, was then Commissioner. They were sort of pushing and shoving, and you could see these coppers were thinking, "Why are these people here? Why are they fighting about the future of Iran in the middle of Manchester?" You could see these very dim coppers trying, "What's going on? What's going on here?" But they were too busy holding the crowds back from killing each other.

This was 30 years ago now. Thatcher, the alleged Right-winger, is in charge of the country. I remember when Leon Brittan came to Manchester University. He's a Jewish internationalist who's in favor of much of the present set-up. But to the Leftist demonstrators he was a Tory, you know, a fascist. And they rioted on the Oxford Road. There was blood all over the front of the union steps. The Greater Manchester Police special patrol group type squad beat them and pushed them back. There was an attempt to storm Brittan's car. When he was interviewed on *News at Ten* later he was quite shaken, you could see it. You know, it was rough business that'd been going on. It was almost a sort of violent comedy.

It's interesting that that radicalism has died down though. I remember you used to go up Oxford Road, and everything that could be posted had a Socialist Workers Party poster on it. You never see them now.

Yes, of course. No. They were all printed in East London by East London Offset because they always used to have those big bars of black, didn't they? SOCIALISM and in big bars of black: THE PEOPLE'S PEACE. REJECT THATCHER'S CUTS. And all the usual stuff.

It's amazing, because this new generation has emerged. It's very tiny now. It's about a tenth of what it was. For every 100 far Leftists in 1980 there's about one now. But a new generation has emerged, and for them, of course, it's a historical symbol. It's like their own revisionism, isn't it? It's their own restorationism of the red, white, and blue.

When Steve and I were trying to get in at about 9 in the morning the mob was gathering. I suddenly noticed they all had these communist flags, and they're all about 20. Because they've never really known what it was like, you see. They were all born in 1990, aren't they really?

[...]

I remember a *Sun* journalist approached me once and said, "What do you think of our *Sun* then?" I said, "It's utter drivel." And I said, "And you're a cretin." And he went, "Oh right, so you're a snob are you?" I said, "I'm far worse than a snob." And he went, "You are? Are you a fascist?" I said, "Well . . . that depends." I was a bit more cautious then. I said, "I've invited Jean-Marie Le Pen to dinner." In that big dinner that Western Goals did in 1991. It was all over the media. He said, "Oh, you *are* a fascist then!" He said, "Will you admit to being a fascist in my column?" I said, "Not yet." And he went, "Oh . . ." [Bowden makes a long, droopy sad face.] But he really was a tabloid journalist. Stained mac, sort of rat-like. He really was sort of almost sub-human. He really was sort of "Ehhh!" The sort that would be outside the widow's door, and the door opens, and he says, "How do ya feel, love?" One of those. A real sort of scumbag. It was so interesting to see what you always thought they were like.

[G.B.] once took me 20 years ago around the newsroom at *The Sun*. Very interesting. "Hello, G——!" and all this. Half of them were upper middle class. They were blokes with dickey bow ties, and they're doing *The Sun*. The other blokes were wide boys and blokes with their bacon sandwiches on the computer and sort of, "All right! Have an effin' good one, mate!" And the next one is a bloke with a bow tie doing *The Sun* and this sort of thing.

It's sort of heavily fortified. When we went in there, because of course they'd had the prints dispute not long before and there was real violence. There was fights at the end where anarchists and heavy mob, early Class War, they all turned up and they were hurling absolute bricks at the police. It really was rioting. They threw acid at the gates. This was heavy duty stuff, because they sacked a whole generation of print workers. Mind you, half of them hadn't done a job for a long time.

You know they used to have ghosting? A bloke used to sign in, and you'd take a mattress into work, "Working's a mug's game, boy!" And they certainly believe that. That's why the economy fell apart in the '70s and why people voted for Thatcher. Because things didn't work. We were heading for Venezuela.

My father would say, "I'm going to vote Thatcher. I don't want to. I think she might be a bit cruel." He's always worried about that sort of militancy which he saw as a bank manager. When in the mid-1980s he'd sit in board meetings and so on and bankers would say, "Crush the unions! It's our revenge for the '60s and '70s and Wilson," and all this nonsense. Sort of unbridled middle class power, really. And he always felt very awkward and sort of queasy about that. "Break the unions!" "Privatize the NHS!" one bloke once said to him. "Make granny pay for her hip!"

And my father was appalled at this, but he was in no sense any sort of a socialist or anything socialistic at all. "I didn't think it was morally right," he said to me. "It's too merciless. I didn't like the cut of their jib," he said. But it's all hesitant and unformed. They regard him as a bloody liberal, wet, a wet Tory in their sense, because they were dry. Drier than dry. It was a reaction to the extreme unionist stuff in the 1970s. "One out, all out!" Yes, "I'm all right, Jack."

Is it really viable to adopt protectionist economic policies when all our natural coal and gas reserves have been depleted for so long?

I think what you do is you adopt attenuated ones. Life is partly a war of position. Total autarky is completely ridiculous. That's Hoxha's Albania. But if you allow yourself to have no industrial base at all and you don't make anything then you are heading for the knacker's yard. I remember Reagan once said, "Oh, we don't need a productive industrial base." What does he think an economy will ultimately be based on if you don't actually physically make anything? Somebody drove me through the industrial districts of Liverpool, and there was one factory making bouncy castles, and that was it.

So, you need a mix. You need to bring things in from outside. You need to exclude foreign influence. You need to manage and manipulate things to your own advantage. Economics is, in part, a form of warfare, and you need to take that attitude. The Japanese and the Chinese have that view. They synthetically adopt different strategies—protectionism, semi-autarky, allow things in, pump priming, militant libertarianism—if they perceive it to be in their national interest at any one time. These are tactics that you use, not shibboleths.

The Friedmans of this world, the Hayeks of this world, and the Keyneses of this world believe that people will go to the barricade for a theory about how the economy should be run. These are just tactics, tactics that governments and statesmen and senior economists and industrialists and capitalists use. You know, George W. Bush has introduced militant state socialist measures to save Western fiscal capitalism. He's adopted measures to the Left of the American Socialist Party, and he's a Republican market militant who's fought those Left-liberal measures all his life. But when it faced collapse the state had to take it over. So, I see economics as a matter of tactics not of morals and not *really* of what politics is about.

In relation to the current economic, environmental, and immigration crisis in the West, if radical political change does not happen what are your predictions?

A mess! And dog eat dog in an unpleasant way, but then life is like that anyway, up to a point. It will be a bang or a whimper as the West moves into the next century and more. Life and mankind's nature abhors a vacuum, so there will always be new forces coming up.

I think it's 1909 writ large a hundred years on. If you stood in 1909, you've got a First World War to come (what a joy!); you've got the Depression to come and the Roaring Twenties before; the reaction to the first war and then the bust that follows it; you've got the rise of fascism and communism; you have a second war; the whole of the last half of the last century is reacting to the devastation of the Second World War, at least within the West; you then have a Cold War, which is hot in the Second and Third World, very much so, but the West is in a state of stasis with the Soviet bloc; you have the unpeeling of Soviet communism, and now we're in a new world where we are.

I think as we sit here in 2009 we face a radical future, a radical future that has many possibilities and many dangers. There's a book called Yockey's *Imperium* written in the middle of the 20th century. I agree with some of it. I don't agree with some of it. It's partial. It's written in its time. Nevertheless, the introduction is written by a man called Willis A. Carto, a veteran of the American far Right, and Carto believed with Spengler that a new authoritarianism would come after collapse, but later he revised his view, a sort of self-revisionism, and he rather worryingly said that [he] thinks it might end in anarchy and in chaos.

And these societies are heading for anarchy. Strangely, socialism moves towards communism and communism moves back towards socialism on the Left flank, but liberalism moves towards anarchism, which is technically to the Left of communism. Forget the anarchist theory, forget even an individualist like Stirner or a social anarchist like Bakunin and [unintelligible] or Kropotkin, forget the theorists. Just sort of chaos and the attempt to keep it from one's door.

If there is not major energies put into cultural and social and national renewal in Western societies, the reality is a sort of negative Venezuela where a rich man's daughter goes to the shops with the blokes next to her with an AK-47, writ large. Private estates, gated estates, private areas that are guarded. It's already well on the way to happening. You know, you swipe a card through one of these devices, and the gate opens. There are security systems all around. People have got hired heavies to go anywhere if they've got anything to protect, namely something to lose, that means somebody can take it off them. If you've got nothing to lose nobody's going to take it off you. So, the rich are always alone and always in fear. The loneliness of the rich.

So, it's sort of *Blade Runner*, really. Fantasies always tell the future. That's what the future will be like unless there's a move for social redemption. Put another way, the redemption will become individual, and individuals who are strong and individuals who can make money and individuals who are intelligent will just subtract, which is the process that is of course well under way. They will subtract from the rest. And they'll just look out for themselves and their families, and they'll be all right, at least they think they will be. And everyone else will be in a sort of pit.

Isn't there a comic called *2000 AD*?

Judge Dredd.

And wasn't there the rival series, the more Left-wing one, *Nemesis*, where the humans are the villains? The humans live in these enormous skyscrapers called termite hills . . . termitescapes . . . termite towers. And there's a man called Torquemada, who's a sort of fascist Catholic sort of thing who runs the whole thing with a big pointy hat. It's all ridiculous, of course. But the idea of these humans living in great blocks milling around and, as Torquemada's first wife says, "Their lives are so unimportant." I think for those who are shut out of capital and great wealth it would be like those urban landscapes in Manchester with the millionaire looking down on the heroin addict.

So, how does a sane person exist in a mad society like that?

Well, you sort of go some place else, I think, or go somewhere else within one's own mind, but people will find a way to exist. Humans are endlessly adaptable. You find your own way. Indeed, that's what people are doing. They've largely privatized their own lives. They've got asocial attitudes. They don't think in political terms anymore. People aren't interested in politics anymore. They're sick of Labour. They just want to get them out and get a new lot in to manage what's going on a little bit better as they perceive it. The reason they want them to better is just because it's a change. It's like someone needs a holiday after a lot of work. Change is as good as a rest. It's not a brilliant way to run a country, but when you allow the masses to decide who should rule in that sort of a way I'm afraid you'll get that.

But life's totally open. Anything can change. A man could have an idea, not with a typewriter anymore now, but with a computer on his own in a room alone, a laptop and the world can change. Everything is possible. Our group believes that it's all open. Everything is still possible. We're here. We've had some nice wine and crisps. It's not always totally as bad as everyone thinks. The changes that need to happen are moral and mental and spiritual. If they happen, enormous changes can occur. If they don't happen, not much will happen.

But I'm an optimist. Most Right-wing people are pessimistic introverts, and I'm an optimistic extrovert. I'm not an individualist in the complete social and philosophical sense at all, because we're all part of society and somebody made these shoes and this tie and even this symbol [his odal rune pendant], you know, we're all sort of interconnected, but I do believe you live your own life, and you have a bit of pleasure on the way. I don't believe in misery. Misery is for bores. I don't believe in that.

So, you wouldn't say optimism is cowardice then?

No. I don't agree with Spengler. Spengler's a classical pessimist. He's an introvert, and he's a great thinker, but he's nervous about the future. Of course, ontologically, the future is death, but one of the first moments in life is to overcome one's fear of death. Most people are terrified of death. They can't even mention it. They're paralyzed. Religion tells you death isn't the end. I don't believe death is the end, but whether there's anything conscious afterwards I don't know, and nobody does.

I believe one's life is a bullet passing through screens and you hit a screen you can't pass through and it's over. So, I believe you go on.

A bishop came to our first meeting. There was a debate afterward where he was asked questions, and somebody said, "Do you believe that God is love?" And he said, "Yes." I wasn't chairman of the New Right then. Jonathan B— was. I put my hand up and said, "If you want to call it God, the divine, the energy in all things, the force that created the universe, nature, whatever you call it, I believe it's fury not love." And he said, "I don't agree." And somebody else said, "But yes, where is the love in your system then?" I said, "Love is creation. If the world's being created by a force and by a force that knows not itself as it does it, that's the greatest form of affection you could ever have, isn't it? To create all this?"

So, I don't believe in misery. You know, most of the other racial groups on this Earth don't believe in misery. I believe one should go forward. It's integration that we need. Stoicism, integration. We've got very miserable ones down in the mouth, and I don't agree with all that. I know things are in quite a mess, but it's because we've adopted views which are counter-productive and views which are destructive and views which can be reversed. If we really decided to reverse them it would all change very quickly. It's whether we really want to or really wish to go through the pain that will be involved in that.

But, you know, woman goes through a lot of pain in giving birth to one child. This always has to be remembered in our male way of looking at things, that there are other forms of strength, there are other forms of power and those are good because they're based on natural processes. There's quite a lot of women involved in Right-wing politics, actually, and that's because they sense there's a danger to their group, and it's instinctual. It's not really theoretical, but it's a response, and that's a good thing.

No, I believe in the future. I'm a progressive, you see, in a strange sort of way. I just want to progress somewhere else. Nietzsche's a progressive who wants to go on with inequality. The modern world's happened. We're in it.

I suppose the best answer is when somebody asked me, "Why do you like modernist art?" And I do, at least in part, whereas most Right-wing people on the whole can't stand it. I said, "Because it's *ferocious!* And because it's here, and we're alive now!" And because it's non-dualist, and because it's purely for intellectuals. That's why the masses don't like it. And because it's sort of energetic and slightly horrid. They said, "Oh, that's not very democratic, is it?" But why? Why *be* democratic?

If I was on the Turner Prize committee, I'd say, "Well, let's take these ten criminals and hang them, and we'll photograph that and we'll make a Turner Prize exhibit with that!" Damien Hirst can stick his thumbprint on the edge of it and say, "It was my idea anyway, mate!" You know, the man who got an E in A-level art and that sort of thing. I'd give them a Turner Prize that they wouldn't like. So, that's my sort of attitude towards things.

Somebody once said to me, "We must blow up the Mandela monument," outside the NFC or wherever it is on the South Bank. The one that was raised to two levels because somebody tried to do that 25 years ago and the other one that was raised by 400,000 pounds of subscription in Parliament Square because, of course, he's become a secular saint. I said, "No, don't do that! Just paint it white and have a dickey bow tie on it with a big red nose, and on Red Nose Day you press a button and the tie goes around and so on", and you've made a mockery of him, you see. You've engaged in *détournement.* You've turned the thing around.

The Right will only defeat the Left and the Center if it's more creative, more energetic, more radical, more intelligent, more sassy, cooler. That's the only way we'll win. The trouble with Right-wing people, on the whole, is they're sort of pessimistic, slightly unimaginative. They're deeply conservative people. They're very decent people, but they're conservative. You've got to be more radical than that.

I'm a very conservative person, but I'm also a revolutionary. You need the two combined, you see. That's why I call myself a revolutionary conservative, which most people think, "What is he talking about?" But it's true. That's what I am really. The irony is when I was in Griffin's party I was by far one of the most Right-wing people in it, and that's not a stupid statement at all. It was strange actually. It went from extreme Tory . . . Because when I turned up many of them thought I'd be an ultra-reactionary in their terms, and I ended up almost an ultra in that party, but in a different way to the others, because they just judge it there's the civic nationalists, the populists, and the nativists, and the fascists. That's the range within the party, if one speaks honestly. I didn't entirely fit into any of those categories.

I think it's good not to. Why do people always want to fit into these categories, these boxes that people have marked before they've even turned up? I don't see the purpose of all that. They've got to find new syntheses, new ways of doing things, new ways of acting and thinking. The Right did that, you see. It was a totally alternative current from 1880 onwards to about 1920. It was also a counter-cultural current. The whole counter-culture in mid-Europe was on that side then. The counter-culture we understand now is the one that fed into the '60s and the gradual movement through the institutions of the Blair generation is the '60s coming to power. Greg Dyke in the BBC, Blair in government. It had all been prefigured by people before, but that's the key generation who are 60 now and were 20 when it was all kicking off in the 1960s. This sort of stuff. A bit different, but that sort of range of ages. Brown is right at the edge of it in age terms. There are younger people still in the Cabinet and seeking to replace them from other parties.

But the '60s revolution is a cultural revolution, not really an economic one, but a cultural and social revolution and it needs to be reversed or changed. The energy can be taken and changed and moved in a new direction, you see? Everything's about energy. Master it, control it, and you can control the world.

Probably a good moment to stop actually.

Studies in Reaction Series: